WHO WANTS TO LIVE FOREVER

QUEEN: LIFE AFTER FREDDIE

MERCURY

Featuring Brian May, Roger Taylor, Adam Lambert &

Paul Rodgers

WHO WANTS TO LIVE FOREVER

QUEEN: LIFE AFTER FREDDIE MERCURY

Featuring Brian May, Roger Taylor, Adam Lambert &

Paul Rodgers

BY

NEIL DANIELS

NEIL DANIELS

Who Wants To Live Forever – Queen: Life After Freddie Mercury

First edition published, 2017

ISBN-13: 978-1544143248

ISBN-10: 1544143249

Visit Createspace at *www.createspace.com*

Visit Neil Daniels at *www.neildanielsbooks.com*

NEIL DANIELS

"I'm Adam onstage. I'm not playing Freddie. I'm not trying to be him. However, he's so amazing. His recordings and his performances were so incredible that I can't help but be inspired by them."

- **Adam Lambert speaking to Daniel Reynolds,** *Advocate*, **2014**

"The thing is he's [Adam Lambert] not Freddie. He doesn't need to be Freddie. Not in any sense is Freddie imitated. Adam has an extraordinary instrument – the most wonderful instrument you could possibly find in this world, you know. There's no dispute in that. He also has an ability with the audience. He has a natural way with the crowd. He is an entertainer."

- **Brian May speaking to Matt Fleming,** *Time Out Hong Kong*, **2016**

"Queen is like one of my all-time favourite rock bands, and then to be up on stage with KISS with the pyro and the costumes – I mean, it was a dream come true. It was awesome."

- **Adam Lambert speaking to Adam B. Vary,** *Entertainment Weekly*, **2009**

"He has a lot of things in common with Freddie Mercury. He has an incredible sense of humour, which is very important, and he has an incredible vocal range. Those two things really make him perfectly fitted for Queen. Brian and I didn't expect to still be working under the name Queen but this is our fourth or fifth tour [with Lambert] and we've found ourselves absolutely loving it."

- **Roger Taylor speaking to Matt Fleming, *Time Out Hong Kong*, 2016**

"Well, it was an interesting thing playing with Queen. I always follow my heart in things, you know. And it's taken me on all kinds of roller coaster rides I must admit (chuckle), and a lot of people say, 'oooh, that sounds like an odd pairing, you with Queen'. And I would have said so myself, frankly, had I not played with them first. We played on a live TV show and we both wanted to play live. And when we came off stage, we just felt, wow that was just so great. Let's do more. And I thought we'll do maybe a couple of shows, just for fun."

- **Paul Rodgers speaking to Morley Seaver, *Anti Music*, 2007**

CONTENTS

INTRODUCTION

Queen are one of the most successful British rock bands of all time with sales estimated to be somewhere between 150 and 300 million. They have won just about every major award possible in the music and entertainment industry. Their origins were in glam rock with touches of prog and heavy metal before they became a fully-fledged stadium rock band in the 1980s. They have influenced amongst others, Guns N' Roses, Van Halen, Foo Fighters, The Smashing Pumpkins, Nirvana, Iron Maiden, Anthrax and Dream Theater et al.

Some of their most famous albums include *A Night At The Opera* (1975), *News Of The World* (1977), *The Game* (1980) and *A Kind Of Magic* (1986). The band was comprised of singer Freddie Mercury, guitarist Brian May, drummer Roger Taylor and bassist John Deacon.

Between 2004 and 2009 Taylor and May reformed Queen (minus the retired Deacon) with Free and Bad Company singer Paul Rodgers. They played two world tours and recorded one album, *The Cosmos Rocks*. Since the Q+PL collaboration the band hooked up with *American Idol* finalist Adam Lambert;

a young and talented singer far more suited to the pomp and grandiosity of Queen's epic musical legacy than Rodgers. Since 2011 Queen have been performing live sold out shows around the world with Lambert. There have been no live releases, though critics have raved about them. They headlined the Isle Of Wight festival in 2016 and generally regarded as the highlight of the weekend.

There have been dozens of books on Queen but this one charts the band's musical output since the death of Freddie Mercury. Some of the band's decisions post-Freddie have been controversial (5ive and Robbie Williams collaborations) and not so well-received (*The Cosmos Rocks*) but it seems that they have finally hit the nail on the head with Lambert whom fans, including me, have certainly warmed to. Roger Taylor and Brian May are still brimming with energy and talent; and it's easy to see why they won't let the band rest even when their former comrade John Deacon has chosen to retire and stay silent. Queen rocks. Still.

Neil Daniels

www.neildanielsbooks.com

NEIL DANIELS

FREDDIE MERCURY TRIBUTE CONCERT & MADE IN HEAVEN: A RECAP

Queen frontman Freddie Mercury died on November 24, 1991; just 24 hours after an official press statement was released confirming that Mercury had AIDS. He died from bronchial pneumonia brought on by AIDS. He was buried in Kensal Green, West London on November 27. The world had lost one of the greatest stage performers of all time; a true showman and extravert.

"It was strange, because none of us really thought he would die," May said to *Goldmine*'s Dave Thompson. "It was unthinkable, although obviously you have the possibility in the back of your head 24 hours a day. It's the most unreal thing to go through with somebody you've been that close with for that long. Having 'The Show Must Go On' out as a single at that time, it was very bizarre, because the way the song came about in the first place was strange."

Regularly voted the greatest frontman of all time, Freddie Mercury fronted Queen from 1970 until his death in 1991. Of the 17 songs featured on Queen's *Greatest Hits* album, he wrote ten: 'Bohemian Rhapsody', 'Seven Seas Of Rhye', 'Killer Queen', 'Somebody To Love', 'Good Old-Fashioned Lover Boy', 'We Are The Champions', 'Bicycle Race', 'Don't Stop Me Now', 'Crazy Little Thing Called Love' and 'Play The Game'. He has posthumously been inducted into the Rock And Roll Hall Of Fame, the Songwriters Hall Of Fame, the UK Music Hall Of Fame and the Hollywood Walk Of Fame. A film based on his life is said to be in development. The legend lives on.

The late music critic and author Harry Doherty was especially close to Queen and covered them extensively. He told the author in 2010: "Queen were just grandiose. Larger than life. And I loved them for that. Plus the fact that they could write pop songs in a rock format. And they knew no fear. Every quarter of that band had a role to play, and they knew that. From the start, they felt it was them against the world."

He continued: "Once they decided they liked you, it was fine. My first interview with them was around the time of *Sheer Heart Attack*. I met Freddie at his PRs and he was explaining in his darling way that Brian couldn't be there because he had time off with hepatitis and now had to catch up on his guitar parts. Freddie was definitely comfortable in his own skin. After that he took me out to dinner after the playback for *A Night At The Opera* to do an interview and meet his gay entourage. 'These are my people', he grandly announced. Brian May was, and still is, deeply suspicious of the press, but we got on very well, and still do. Roger Taylor was a real rock and roller and very approachable. John Deacon kept himself off-limits. The band asked me to do the sleeve notes for the *Live In Ukraine* DVD that Q+PR released last year (2009) so I guess we got on well."

On Mercury's death Doherty said: "Desperately sad, but everybody could see it coming. I had an idea he wasn't well and I thought that when *Innuendo* came out that it would be the last album. The signs were all over that album in the lyrics."

To celebrate Mercury's life and music Queen's most famous song 'Bohemian Rhapsody' was reissued as a single as a double A-side with the moving and sombre 'These Are The Days Of Our Lives', the music video to which was the last time Mercury appeared on camera. He looked frail and gaunt; recorded in May 1991 during his final months. It was terribly sad to see him this way. The single peaked at Number 1 in the

UK. Proceeds from the release went to the AIDS charity, Terrence Higgins Trust. Queen saw a resurgence of popularity in the US after the release of the comedy movie *Wayne's World* which featured the now iconic "driving scene" with 'Bohemian Rhapsody' as the scene's soundtrack. As such 'Bohemian Rhapsody' went to Number 2 in America and helped win the band an MTV Award in 1992. A compilation called *Classic Queen* was released in the US to capitalise on their popularity Stateside. Needless to say the band were more than pleased with *Wayne's World* and thanked actor/writer Mike Myers.

In the UK the band released *Greatest Hits II* in October 1991; a collection as worthy as its best-selling predecessor.

AllMusic's Stephen Thomas Erlewine wrote: "Generally, the songs here favour melodrama to untrammelled rock & roll, which means while there's nothing here that hits as hard as 'Tie Your Mother Down'; there's also nothing as light on its feet as 'Crazy Little Thing Called Love', either. This is not necessarily a bad thing: nobody scaled the dramatic heights like Queen, and this captures their pomp & circumstance at its most polished."

The Freddie Mercury Tribute Concert was held on

April 20, 1992 at London's Wembley Stadium with 72,000 people in attendance and over a billion people watching the concert on their TV's. The concert featured a "who's who" of popular music: Guns N' Roses, Elton John, Metallica, Def Leppard, David Bowie, Annie Lennox, George Michael, Robert Plant, Roger Daltry, Seal and Extreme. The performance of the night was undoubtedly Queen and George Michael (RIP) performing 'Somebody To Love'. The concert raised over 20 million for AIDS charities and was listed in the Guinness Book Of Records as the largest rock star benefit concert ever staged. Freddie would have been proud.

Four years after Freddie Mercury's death during which time Brian May embarked on a solo career, the three remaining members – May, Roger Taylor and John Deacon – regrouped to finish what would be Queen's final album with Mercury, *Made In Heaven*.

Taylor and Deacon actually began the painstaking job of making *Made In Heaven* without May who was busy on tour in support of his solo album (to be discussed in the next chapter. "I was very resistant to anything like that for a long time," he said to *Goldmine*'s Dave Thompson. "I was the bad guy in the sense of doing anything under the Queen banner. I was dragged kicking and screaming into the idea. I really didn't want to make it in the beginning. It was only when I'd heard what Roger and John had done that I rushed in there in my usual arrogant manner and said, 'Stop! You're doing it all wrong.' And once I'd plunged in, it was just massive. It was a couple of years of total dedication to reconstructing and re-creating the Dead Sea Scrolls."

He continued: "It was a terribly demanding job making that album because obviously your brief is to make it sound like it was no trouble at all. It was spun out of thin air and a few little snatches of tape. It was a projection, an extrapolation - what would it have sounded like if Freddie had still been alive and we were really here making this album? Because it wasn't only a matter of what we played, it was the construction of the songs because that never stays the same as you're working on it. A song develops, and if you develop it beyond the point where Freddie's singing, you're in big trouble. It was very tricky, but having found it very painful at the time and for some time after it came out, I now love it. I think it's a really good bit of work."

The album used some of Mercury's final recordings

and songs from their solo albums such as May's 'Too Much Love Will Kill You'. 'Mother Love' was Mercury's last ever recording. He was too ill to return to the studio to finish it so May recorded the final verse.

The album was recorded through its various stages at the band's studio in Montreux, Switzerland.

To celebrate Mercury's life and music, a statue was erected in his honour overlooking Lake Geneva. It was unveiled on November 25, 1996.

Made In Heaven was a Number 1 hit in the UK and went on to shift over 20 million copies worldwide. Not Queen's greatest album; it is still a moving and powerful tribute to the band's late singer.

The Times said: "[There are not] any obviously half-baked, or patched-up numbers. Most, however, are as good as anything that Queen came up with in their later years. How good that is, as always with Queen, is largely a matter of taste. 'Mother Love', the last recording that Mercury made, is a song of truly heartfelt pathos. Despite its overdue delivery, *Made In Heaven* stands up remarkably well as the closing chapter in a spectacular pop odyssey."

The Guardian stated: "When a band have the controls permanently set at full-tilt, as Queen did, burn-out is inevitable, for the listener, if not for the band. When we eventually reach the drum-crashing finale, 'It's A Beautiful Day', which kicks in with Mercury's umpteenth randy-rottweiler howl, it feels as if far more than 70 minutes has passed. That's where the aforesaid lyrics save the day. Predominantly written by Mercury, they are effectively farewell notes. He poured out his heart, and his words have a throat-aching poignance. Even the record's opening verse assumes a painful significance."

Q Magazine said: "No filler. No shame. An essential purchase for Queen fans, certainly, but even without its special significance, *Made In Heaven* is probably a better album than Innuendo and a fitting swan song by one of the most incandescent groups in rock. *Made In Heaven* is also the last musical will and testament of a star who was never going to be turned into a saint, but whose grandstanding performances were, right to the very end, always marked by reckless enthusiasm and a rare generosity of spirit."

To celebrate Mercury and to remember all those singers who had died too young, May, Taylor and Deacon recorded 'No-

One But You (Only The Good Die Young)' in 1997. It was issued as a single and included as a bonus track on the *Queen Rocks* compilation.

Of the compilation AllMusic's Stephen Thomas Erlewine said: "*Rocks, Vol. 1* is a bit of a hodgepodge and one that most fans will be able to ignore. But for casual fans of Brian May's searing, melodic guitar, Mercury's operatic wail, and the surprisingly swinging backbeat of John Deacon and Roger Taylor, this compilation will suit their needs quite nicely."

Queen performed 'The Show Must Go On' with Elton John at the Bejart Ballet in Paris in January 1997, which was the last time John Deacon appeared in public. May and Taylor, however, missed performing live. They attended and performed together at various ceremonies throughout the 1990s.

In 1998, the pair performed with the legendary Italian Tenor Luciano Pavarotti at his benefit concert. They played 'Too Much Love Will Kill You' with Pavarotti and 'Radio Ga Ga', 'We Will Rock You' and 'We Are The Champions' with Zucchero. They later performed with Pavarotti at another benefit concert of the Tenor's in Modena, Italy in May 2003.

In 1999 Queen released what some would say was an

unnecessary *Greatest Hits III* as it gobbled together various collaborations: a rap version of 'Another One Bites The Dust' with Wyclef Jean, the tribute concert live recording of 'Somebody To Love' with George Michael and a live recording of 'The Show Must Go On' with Elton John. While Deacon chose not to continue with Mercury it seemed that May and Taylor just could not let the band go. They were one of the biggest-selling bands of all time, only second to The Beatles.

Classic Rock said of the collection: "…there are some gems. The reworked 'Another One Bites The Dust' with Wyclef Jean of the Fugees is ace, demonstrating once again just how far the band could stretch their sound. And the live version of 'The Show Must Go On' with Elton John on vocals is even more poignant than Freddie's original. If you can imagine such a thing."

Chester Chronicle said: "It is eight years since the release of Queen's previous *Hits II*, and eight years since Freddie Mercury's death, yet still this new, and inevitably final, collection of 17 tracks is able to justify the 'hits' title - all, with the exception of the new 'The Show Must Go On', have continued Queen's unbroken run in the charts, four of them reaching number one."

Various collaborative recordings happened in the early noughties: Queen recorded 'We Will Rock You' with the pop band 5ive and 'We Are The Champions' with ex Take That Robbie Williams which was included in the soundtrack for the Heath Ledger movie *A Knight's Tale* in 2003. Queen had sold out and rock fans were left aghast.

May spoke to *Goldmine*'s Dave Thompson about the Williams collaboration: "We just got in and played it. It was a good experience all 'round because it wasn't synthetic. We actually did get in there and play it with him, and he sang it live like the trouper that he is. He's a good boy, Robbie. He's really turned it around. He comes from a place in [U.K. boy band sensation] Take That [that] I don't think any of us would admit had any worth, and then gradually you just had to admit that the guy has talent. I had a very strong feeling about him from a few years ago, ever since I saw a video of his performance at Slane Castle. He's one of the very few people today who can really entertain an audience. He can really capture them in the palm of his hand. He's very different from Freddie, but he has that common touch in common. He can send himself up, he can have a laugh, but at the same time he can gather the whole thing up and deliver a performance which is arresting."

Nevertheless they had been awarded a star on the Hollywood Walk Of Fame which May and Taylor attended on October 18, 2002. Fans can check it out at 6358 Hollywood Blvd.

May and Taylor performed at the 46664 Concert hosted by Nelson Mandela at Green Point Stadium in Cape Town on November 29, 2003. The concert was especially important to the band as it was to help raise awareness of HIV and AIDS in South Africa. May and Taylor were made ambassadors for the 46664 charity.

Both May and Taylor like to keep busy especially May who seems to have boundless energy and passion for both music and non-musical projects (being a noted scientist). They even found time to work on solo projects.

SOLO WORK

"Roger and John and I are very good friends still and socially we're probably better friends than we ever were," May admitted to CNN's *World Beat* in 2000. "But we like, we all like to do things in a different way now. You know, we were part of this great team for all those years but there's a certain benefit in not being in a team in that way anymore and I think we've all found our freedom to an extent since Queen was no longer a going concern. The nice thing about Queen is that Queen never got old. I'm getting old, but Queen doesn't get old."

The 1990s also saw May and Taylor explore solo careers while Deacon quietly retired. He released his first two solo albums in the 1980s taking time out from Queen while his comrades also pursued projects: *Fun In Space* came out in 1981 with *Strange Frontier* hitting the record shelves in 1984.

Taylor with his band The Cross released their third and final album *Blue Rock* in 1991 (following 1988's *Shove It*, 1990's *Mad, Bad and Dangerous to Know*.) He then released three albums under his own name: *Happiness* in 1994, *Electric Fire* in 1998 and then more recently, *Fun On Earth* in 2013.

"It's been a long time since my last album and it's taken me a long time to make it," Taylor said to *Something Else Reviews* of *Fun On Earth*. "It's been labour of love over four or five years really. It's an accumulation of material that I've had that I've wanted to get off my chest. I've got a really great studio here at home, so it's been really nice for me to go into my studio for a bit and work on my thing in between the rest of the projects Queen tend to be doing."

William S. Clark IV of *Music Enthusiast Mag* said of the album: "However, songs such as the closing track 'Smile' are right in line with something one would expect from a Roger Taylor-fronted Queen outtake, with bold vocal harmonies greeting the listener. Just about the only way this song in particular could sound more at home on a new Queen release is if Brian May joined Taylor on vocals. The same can also be said for 'One Night Stand', which more closely resembles what one could anticipate out of a 'I'm In Love With My Car' B-side. In many ways *Fun On Earth* is exactly what fans could expect from a 2013 Roger Taylor solo album, and at the same time also shows the Queen drummer reigniting the liberty of being a musician and exploring new musical horizons."

Fireworks rock magazine writer and designer James Gaden is a huge Roger Taylor and Queen fan. Here, he discusses Taylor's solo career in detail:

"Roger Taylor was the first member of Queen to strike out and try his hand as a solo artist. He took the first tentative steps in 1977, issuing the single 'I Wanna Testify', a heavily re-written and rearranged cover of The Parliaments track, with Taylor performing all of the instruments and vocals himself. Backed with a self-penned original 'Turn On The TV', the single was not a hit but did see Taylor make some TV appearances to promote it.

His first solo album would come in 1981, entitled *Fun In Space*. A collection of ten original cuts, described by Taylor as 'an album full of songs that I knew couldn't be done with Queen. I don't know why they were not suitable for us as a band, they just weren't.' Once again, Taylor handled all of the guitars, bass, drums and vocals while sharing keyboard duties with engineer David Richards. A quirky album with a loose Sci-Fi theme, it was well received, charting at Number 18 in the UK.

A second full length album would arrive in 1984, entitled *Strange Frontier*. 'The nuclear threat seemed real and looming at the time and as a father of young children I felt it as a terrible threat to the future' was how Taylor described the subject matter of the title-track. It was released as a single, although the video, based on James Dean's *Rebel Without A Cause* had to be cut to omit the scene of what some people perceived to be a child in an exploding building. The catchy 'Man On Fire' was also released with a promotional video, while the album itself differed from its predecessor by including two cover versions and some guest appearances. Taylor recorded versions of Bruce Springsteen's 'Racing In The Street' and Bob Dylan's 'Masters Of War', and co-wrote 'It's An Illusion' with Status Quo's Rick Parfitt, who plays guitar and sings backing vocals on the track. Taylor's Queen band mate John Deacon delivered a superb remix of 'I Cry For You' (which showed hints of where 'Radio Ga Ga' would come from later that year on Queen's *The Works* album) and Freddie Mercury was rumoured to have sung backing vocals on 'Killing Time', although this is unconfirmed. The album charted at Number 30 in the UK, and a couple of non-album tracks also appeared from these sessions: the oddball 'Two Sharp Pencils' which appeared as the B-side to *Strange Frontier* and a cover of the Spencer Davis Group's 'Keep On Running' which can be heard in demo form online, but has never been officially released.

After Queen had completed their huge tour in support of *A Kind Of Magic* each member took time away from their parent band. Taylor decided his next move would be to form a new group, which he entitled The Cross, with a plan to be in a working band to play live when Queen were on hiatus. The Cross would co-exist with Queen, at no point interfering with Taylor's main group. Placing an anonymous advert in the music press to recruit hungry young musicians, Taylor eventually settled on bassist Peter Noone, guitarist Clayton Moss, and drummer Josh McCrae. Keyboards would be handled by long time Queen sideman Spike Edney, and Taylor assumed responsibility for rhythm guitar and lead vocals.

The Cross made their debut with *Shove It!*, effectively a Taylor solo record in all but name. He had already written and recorded the bulk of the songs himself, but wanting to get the new members to input themselves into the group, parts of the album were re-recorded. The record was a hybrid of pop and rock music, cleverly weaving in dance orientated beats with rock guitars. Queen band mates Brian May and Freddie Mercury appeared on the album, with May delivering some trademark guitar work on 'Love Lies Bleeding' while Mercury performed lead vocals on 'Heaven For Everyone', and track that would later be re-worked by Queen for the *Made In Heaven* release. The Cross played a 16 date tour to support the record, including a handful of TV appearances, as well as releasing singles 'Cowboys And Indians', 'Heaven For Everyone' (the single version featuring Taylor on lead vocals instead of Mercury) and the title-track itself, which made clever use of Queen samples. This was backed with a non-album track 'Feel The Force' but none of the singles performed particularly well, and the album stalled at Number 58.

After a single only track 'Manipulator', written by Taylor, Edney and Steve Strange from Visage, Taylor had to leave The Cross to their own devices while he was busy working with Queen on what would become *The Miracle*. The remaining four members did not sit idle, and when the second album *Mad, Bad And Dangerous To Know* landed, it was notable for a distinct change in sound and a lack of Taylor's writing – he contributed just two songs, the political rocker 'Old Men Lay Down' and the excellent ballad 'Final Designation', and co-wrote the opening rocker 'Top Of The World Ma' with the other four members. The rest of the material, save for a sturdy cover of Jimi Hendrix's 'Foxy Lady', came from the rest of the group. Clayton Moss stepped up to take lead vocals on the gentle 'Better Things' while the impressive 'Power To Love', penned by Noone, Moss and McCrae, was selected as a single. An entertaining promotional video was made which showed off The Cross as a much harder rocking unit, with more guitars and a lot less of the pop influences. A second single, the more commercial 'Liar' featured a video consisting of mostly live footage and was backed with a great non-album track 'In Charge Of My Heart'. A change of record label from Virgin to Electrola in Germany made sense as Germany was becoming the band's strongest market, and the group toured there to a relatively enthusiastic response, but it was at the expensive of promotion in the UK and the album did not chart. A final single was released, with 'Final Destination' being put out backed by The Cross performing 'Man Of Fire' live.

A year later The Cross would deliver their third album, *Blue Rock.* Arguably the most cohesive of the band's three albums, it saw Edney get heavily involved, grabbing writing credits on no less than seven of the ten original tracks. Taylor composed the melancholy 'The Also Rans' and the popular 'New Dark Ages' which was chosen as the single. The Cross had completed a whistle stop tour of Germany supporting Magnum (who Taylor had produced for their *Vigilante* album) in September 1991 to coincide with the album's release, but the death of Freddie Mercury saw interest in the album dissipate, and it was only released in Germany and Japan. The Cross played at the London Astoria at Christmas time, joined by Brian May and ex-Smile colleague Tim Staffell for the encores, and then played their final gig in Gosport in 1993.

Taylor returned to solo work in 1994 with the downbeat but excellent *Happiness*? album. Recorded at his home in Surrey, Taylor brought in guitarist Jason Falloon, bassist Phil Spalding and keyboard player Mike Crossley to augment his vision and enlisted in his former colleague from The Cross, Josh McCrae, to co-produce. The first single was a protest song 'Nazis 1994' which charted at Number 22, despite it being banned by Radio 1. The video was also banned due to its scenes of war and images of the holocaust. Several remixes of the song were issued as singles, with at least a couple of them being arguably better than the album version. The second single was a collaboration with X Japan's Yoshiki, a skilled concert pianist and accomplished rock drummer. The resulting track 'Foreign Sand' was an excellent string and piano laden power ballad which charted at Number 26 and was backed with a brilliant re-working of 'Final Destination'. The album was also notable for the inclusion of 'Old Friends', which Taylor wrote in remembrance of Mercury. The album charted at Number 22 in the UK.

To promote *Happiness?* Taylor undertook his first ever solo tour, backed by Falloon, Crossley, McCrae and Stuart Bradley on bass. Taylor handled lead vocals, as well as additional percussion on a second drum kit set up on stage, plus some additional guitar. The tour took in the UK, Japan, Germany and Italy and saw Taylor perform the bulk of the *Happiness?* material, dust off 'Man On Fire' and include several Queen tracks, such as 'Ride The Wild Wind', 'A Kind Of Magic', 'Radio Ga Ga', 'I Want To Break Free', 'These Are The Days Of Our Lives', 'We Will Rock You', 'I'm In Love With My Car', 'The Show Must Go On' and 'Tenement Funster'. The song 'Happiness?' was released as a single and was backed with some live tracks taken from a show at the Shepherd's Bush Empire.

Four years later Taylor would release *Electric Fire*, and album which he described as 'The most underrated of all my efforts'. Unlike *Happiness?, Electric Fire* covered a variety of tempos and styles, from upbeat rock like 'A Nation Of Haircuts' and 'No More Fun' to tender ballads like 'Tonight'. Retaining Falloon on guitar, Crossley on keys and McCrae as co-producer, Taylor added the superb female vocalist Treana Morris, who had issued a largely ignored solo album before being spotted by the Queen percussionist. She contributed her inimitable vocals to 'Surrender' and 'London Town (C'mon Down)', her angelic voice meshing beautifully with Taylor's more soulful tones. Another cover, John Lennon's 'Working Class Hero' was included. The single 'Pressure On' was issued, with 'Surrender' as a follow up. The album charted at Number 53.

Taylor performed a live concert at the 'Cyberbarn' located at his home in Surrey, where his group played live in front of a privately invited audience and the concert was streamed on the internet, a rarity back in 1998. Attracting over 595,000 hits, it resulted in an entry in the Guinness Book Of

Records for the largest internet audience for an event. The concert was released on VHS and Taylor then embarked on a 16 date UK tour to promote *Electric Fire*, again opting to play the bulk of the album, include some Queen material and add in 'Happiness?', 'Man On Fire' and 'Strange Frontier'. Treana Morris opened the show and would join Taylor on stage for some of the 'Electric Fire' songs and an impressive duet of Queen's 'Under Pressure'. A new single of 'Pressure On' was also released in aid of the Manchester United Supporters Club, with Taylor putting aside his support for Chelsea in order to thwart the attempts of Rupert Murdoch (who Taylor had targeted on the *Happiness?* album) from buying the Red Devils.

The only thing close to a solo release after that was a reggae styled single credited to Felix and Arty called 'Woman… You're So Beautiful' in 2006, which turned out to be Roger on all instruments and his eldest son Felix handling vocals. All was quiet with fifteen years passing before another solo album appeared.

2013 saw the arrival of *Fun On Earth*, which is probably the best album to show off the many facets and talents Taylor possesses. From the simple rocker 'One Night Stand' to the gentle 'Quality Street', the thought provoking 'Fight Club', the protest of 'The Unblinking Eye', a love song 'Be My Gal (My Brightest Spark)' or the humour of 'I Am A Drummer (In A Rock N' Roll Band)' this has something for everyone. 'Small' originally appeared on the Queen + Paul Rodgers album *The Cosmos Rocks*, as did a version of 'Say It's Not True', the rendition here benefitting from guitar work by Jeff Beck. 'Be With You' is also notable for being the first co-write between Taylor and his son Rufus (who has become a good drummer in his own right).

Fun On Earth charted at Number 69, and was released in tandem with a spectacular box set called *The Lot* which featured each of Taylor's five solo albums, and all three albums by The Cross, all remastered and beautifully packaged, along with a DVD containing various promotional videos and live footage, and the various singles and B-sides collected across four discs. *The Lot* also featured some additional tracks for *Fun On Earth*, most notably 'Whole House Rocking' which was re-worked into the title-track for *The Cosmos Rocks*.

That same year, The Cross would reunite to celebrate their 20th Anniversary with a special one off gig in Guildford, where Spike Edney's SAS Band were performing. They delivered a 12 song set which saw each member, with the exception of McCrae, sing lead vocals on a track, with Taylor singing the remainder.

In 2014 Taylor issued a compilation simply titled *Best* where he personally selected 18 tracks from his five solo albums to act as an overview of his prolific career outside of Queen."

Moving on...

Mercury, meanwhile, released *Mr. Bad Guy* in 1985 and *Barcelona* (with Montserrat Caballé) in 1988. Various compilations of his solo work, both released and previously unreleased material, has been issued since his death most notably: 2006's *Lover Of Life, Singer Of Songs - The Very Best Of Freddie Mercury Solo* and 2016's *Messenger Of The Gods: The Singles.* Surprisingly Mercury's solo work is far less interesting than both May and Taylor's.

Brian May has had a shorted but more high profile solo career since Mercury's death.

May first began exploring solo projects in 1983.

He recorded a mini album called *Star Fleet Project* on April 21 and 22 at the famed Record Plant in Los Angeles. The project was dubbed "Brian May + Friends" and features none other than Eddie Van Halen as well as REO Speedwagon drummer Alan Gratzer, session bassist Phil Chen (Jeff Beck and Rod Stewart), session keyboard player Fred Mandel who'd played additional keyboards on Queen's *Hot Space* World Tour and *The Works* and Queen drummer Roger Taylor providing backing vocals on the title-track.

May spoke to *Faces* in 1984 about working with Eddie Van Halen and others: "It was wonderful – the whole couple of days was one of the best experiences of my life. Such a great feeling to play with people who were excited to play with me! That's a feeling I haven't had for a long time. So I didn't care if it sold – I didn't even think it would make it to an album I just wanted to have a tape for myself."

The recording tapes were not supposed to be released by May was urged by his collaborators to release the opus. The recordings had very little mixing.

The project was released in October as a mini LP channeling the conventional full length album and maxi single. The opus consists of 'Star Fleet', 'Let Me Out' and 'Blues Breaker'. 'Star Fleet' was released as a single in 1983 and featured the B-side 'Son Of Star Fleet' which is an instrumental version of the lead song.

The title-track itself and for the album was originated by May's son, Jimmy. It was influenced by the kids' sci-fi series *Star Fleet* which had Japanese effects and British soundtrack with music by Paul Bliss. May became a big fan of the series via his son. 'Let Me Out', on the other hand, was an old song May had in his archives but had yet to record. 'Blues Breaker' was dedicated to Eric Clapton who was an inspiration to May and Van Halen. Hearing May and Van Halen jam together is a treat to the ears. If only they had recorded together again! The mini album was initially released on vinyl but gained a CD released as part of May's 'Back To The Light' single and in 1993 in Japan as part of the mini album *Resurrection*.

May spoke to *Guitar Player* in 1983 about the project: "There weren't any reservations from the other musicians as far as releasing *Star Fleet Project*. Everyone was very positive and has been wonderful to me. In the beginning I didn't want to put it out because I thought it was private, and I didn't know if it would be in good taste to release it. I played it to a few friends, and they said, 'Really, you should, because a lot of people would like to hear this stuff'. So I spoke to each other of the guys individually, and they all said, 'Hey, do what you want with it. We'll be happy'. The only thing which was really hard was getting the paper-work done. These days people's contracts are such complete maze. It took literally a couple of months to get through all the paperwork that was necessary from management and record companies. And that's with the best will in the world; nobody was trying to make it difficult. Queen was leaving Elektra at the time, which was the final piece we had to get into place before we could put anything out. It's a big headache, but I think it's worth it. I want people to know that this is just a one-off thing, a piece of fun. It's not like anyone's leaving their group or anything; there's no hint of that. We're all very much involved with our bands activities. This was just a little trip out."

The album's credits run as Brian May (guitar, vocals, production), Eddie Van Halen (guitar, backing vocals), Alan Gratzer (drums), Phil Chen (bass), Fred Mandel (keyboards), Roger Taylor (backing vocals) with producer Mack, and engineer Mike Beiriger and Nick Froome, additional engineer.

Greg Prato of *All Music* says of the project: "It doesn't take a genius to predict that *Star Fleet* would be a guitar-heavy album, and it is, with lots of over the top guitar duels and songs based on soloing rather than memorable compositions. Still, the title-track rocks like few Queen numbers did in the early '80s, kicking off with Van Halen's signature two-handed tapping technique, and eventually leading into a guitar solo fest. The remaining tracks, 'Let Me Out' and 'Blues Breaker', are blues-based rather than rooted in heavy metal."

May's first production job was Heavy Pettin's debut album *Lettin' Loose* from 1983. It looked as though the Scottish band were going to be the next big attraction in British heavy metal but they never truly took off.

"I really liked their demo and as I'd never produced any other band," May explained to *Faces* in 1984. "I figured I should really do this now or I never would. They reminded me of ourselves, starting out – talented, a proper group in all ways, but not recorded. So I felt I could give them my experience and perhaps prevent many of the difficulties we endured."

In 1986 he contributed to former Genesis guitarist Steve Hackett's album *Feedback 86*.

May played guitar on 'Cassandra' and 'Slot Machine' which he also added vocals to and co-wrote. The album was shelved and finally released in 2000. The album also features Bonnie Tyler and Ian Mosley and Pete Trewavas of Marillion.

In 1986 May also collaborated with his second wife, actress Anita Dobson. Dobson sang vocals to the *EastEnders* theme tune, which became the track 'Anyway Can Fall In Love'. The song, produced by composer Simon May who is behind some of TV's most well-known themes such as *EastEnders* and *Howard's Way*, reached Number 4 in the UK Top 40 singles chart in August.

Dobson's album *Talking Of Love* was released in 1987.

May continued to contribute to other artists work during Queen's career: in 1989 he played guitar solos on the Black Sabbath track 'When Death Calls' which features on their fourteenth studio album *Headless Cross*. Black Sabbath guitarist and band leader Tony Iommi and May are good friends. May also played guitar on the British band Living In A Box song 'Blow The House Down' which features on their 1989 opus *Gatecrashing*.

After the death of Freddie Mercury in November 1991 Brian May was obviously distraught and depressed so he threw himself back into work by working on his first full length solo album *Back To The Light*.

May had begun to work on some solo material in 1988 when both Freddie Mercury and Roger Taylor were working on their own side projects. There was no pressure for him to release the album and without a record deal he worked on the music in his own time between 1988 and 1992 at his home studio in Allerton Hill, Surrey and various studios such as Mountain, Sarm East, Townhouse Studios, Mono Valley and Marcus Studios.

Back To The Light was a transition album.

"Well I think making the *Back To The light* album was the most difficult thing I ever did and it was a big mountain to climb, because it had to be the right quality after all those years with Queen," May reflected to Poland's Radio 3 in 1998. "I had great people to interact with, so making the first album required the greatest strength, I suppose. That was a milestone for me."

Aside from using selected sessions musicians May played many of the instruments himself. Those musicians were Cozy Powell (drums on 'Back To The Light', 'Love Token', 'Resurrection', 'Nothin' But Blue', 'I'm Scared' and 'Driven By You'; new version for US release); Geoff Dugmore (drums on

'Let Your Heart Rule Your Head' and 'Rollin' Over'); Gary Tibbs (bass guitar on 'Back To The Light', 'Let Your Heart Rule Your Head' and 'Rollin' Over'); Neil Murray (bass guitar on 'Love Token', 'I'm Scared' and ' for US release); John Deacon (bass guitar on 'Nothin' But Blue'); Mike Moran (piano on 'Love Token' and 'Rollin' Over', keyboards on 'Last Horizon'); Don Airey (extra keyboards on 'Resurrection' and 'Nothin' But Blue'); Miriam Stockley (backing vocals on 'Back To The Light' and 'Rollin' Over'); Maggie Ryder (backing vocals on 'Back To The Light' and 'Rollin' Over'); Suzie O'List (backing vocals on 'Back To The Light' and 'Let Your Heart Rule Your Head'); Gill O'Donovan (backing vocals on 'Back To The Light' and 'Let Your Heart Rule Your Head') and Chris Thompson (co-lead vocals on 'Rollin' Over').

May spoke to Kirk Blows of *RCD Magazine* in 1992 about the album's emotional impact on him: "There's quite a bit, I suppose, you'd have to fish it out quite carefully. Some of it's quite ambiguous; when I used to listen to Dylan and John Lennon I'd get a piece of life from them that meant something to me. 'Nothin' But Blue' happened because Cozy came in with a backing track and said play something on it. It was the night before Freddie went, but for the first time I had this complete conviction that it was imminent, and I felt that he was going at that point. I used that track and wrote the song about how I felt at that point."

Some songs had been recorded for Queen as demos but were not suitable such as 'The Dark' from the *Flash Gordon* sessions and 'My Boy' during the *Hot Space* era. The initial selection of songs recorded in 1988 were 'Back To The Light', 'I'm Scared', 'Let Your Heart Rule Your Head', 'Too Much Love Will Kill You', 'Last Horizon' and 'Rollin' Over'. The rest of the final album was recorded between 1991 and 1992.

May spoke about the album to *Billboard* in 1993: "When I started this album five years ago, I was severely depressed. I had split from my wife and kids, which was unthinkable. I had lost my father. Also, Queen had stopped touring. All three of these things combined had a tremendous impact on me."

Some of the songs have an interesting genesis.

'Too Much Love Will Kill You' was written when May was living in Los Angeles in the mid-'80s during a complicated time in his personal life. He wrote the song with singer/songwriter Elizabeth Lamers and songwriter Frank Musker whom he met across the pond. Since then a Queen myth has circulated that Lamers gave a demo cassette of the song to a hotel bell boy; said demo is now referred to as 'The Bell Boy Tape', which is also said to contain 'Sleepy Blues' and 'Moody Keyboards'.

'Let Your Heart Rule Your Head' was written around 1988 for skiffle legend Lonnie Donegan at his request for an album that was never released. May kept the song in his archive.

Due to his then highly-publicised rumoured relationship with Anita Dobson (he was still married to Crissie Mullen; the couple would divorce in 1988 and May married Dobson in 2000) May appeared regularly in the British tabloid press, that coupled with the death of his father on June 2 1988, prompted him to write the tracks 'Scandal' and 'I Want It All' which he gave to Queen for *The Miracle* album, released in 1989. 'Too Much Love Will Kill You' was also presented to Queen and appeared on their final album *Made In Heaven*, released after Mercury's death. May, of course, recorded his own version. He also performed live at the Freddie Mercury Tribute Concert at Wembley Stadium in 1992.

The breakdown of his marriage, his private life exposed by the press, the death of his father and Mercury's illness sent May into a depression. He sought some kind of release in his work.

May told *Record Collector* magazine at the time: "Most of the time I've been working on my own. The solo project is mainly about getting all the stuff I've had in my head onto tape, but I've found that some of the ideas I had in mind for solo work have ended up on the Queen album. I think that the best ideas should really be concentrated towards the group, because it's still the best vehicle I can find – as the group is so good!

He continued: "To describe the material is quite difficult. I put the songs on one tape in a very rough form and thought, 'Where am I?', because they are so varied, more so even than Queen material. I've got ballads which are very soft and personal, and I've got stuff which is very hard, pure heavy metal. There are weird acoustic songs, and God knows what else! There isn't a direction to the album yet, and I think that's one problem that I have to sort out."

The UK tracklisting ran as follows: 'The Dark', 'Back To The Light', 'Love Token', 'Resurrection', 'Too Much Love

Will Kill You', 'Driven By You', 'Nothin' But Blue', 'I'm Scared', 'Last Horizon', 'Let Your Heart Rule Your Head', 'Just One Life' and the Small Faces cover, 'Rollin' Over'.

May spoke to *High Voltage* magazine in 1993 about the album title: "First, there's total blackness, and then there's light at the end of the tunnel, and points where you see inspiration in someone else's life. If the album is appreciated by people who are into what I'm into, then that will be enough. Everything else will be a bonus."

The release of the album was prompted by the track 'Driven By You' which was used as the soundtrack to a Ford cars advert in mid-1991.

"It was a kind of fortunate thing," May said to Paul Cashmere of *Undercover* in 1998. "A lot of stuff tends to happen in my life by accident. I had just met these guys one day beside a swimming pool and they asked if I had ever made music for a commercial. I told them no, and they asked me if I wanted to and I said 'no' beaming 'I don't think so'. I considered it something purely commercial and not artistic. They then said 'listen, what have you got to loose. We'll throw a phrase at you see what you come up with'. So I said 'OK, I'll try it' just as an exercise. And it happened very easily."

Queen fans had no knowledge of the song and were annoyed that it sounded remarkably similar to Queen until they discovered it was actually by Brian May.

"See, I thought advertising was a dirty word, and I didn't want much to do with it," he explained further to *Guitar World* in 1993. "But these ad guys threw some slogans at me and I thought, 'Well, I can do it if I relate it to my own experiences and my own feelings.' And the phrase 'Driven By You' immediately jumped out as a description of the way I saw the power struggle between two people in a relationship. It just poured out. I wrote a version for me, and I wrote a version for the ad people. And it worked out great. It was a good kick up the backside for me too, because these people work quickly and do high quality work. On English television, the adverts are a lot better than the programming."

Despite May's initial reluctance to join the advertising world he crafted a solid rock song for Ford Motors.

He spoke about the song title and its genesis to David Mead of *Guitarist* in 1992: "Anyway, they came up with this slogan, which originally was 'Everything We Do, We Do For

You' which was uncannily similar to the Bryan Adams song, which came out a little while afterwards. I thought it sounded a bit slushy and didn't really relate to it. But then they came back and said it was changed to 'Everything We Do Is Driven By You' and my initial thought was 'Yuk, I don't think I can do anything with that either,' because it just sounded like motor cars and I'm not interested in singing songs about motor cars. But then I thought 'Driven By You...' and ping! the lights went on."

The song was set to be released as a single (reportedly with Freddie Mercury's blessing) on November 25 1991 but was delayed by a week as Mercury died on November 24. The single peaked at Number 6 in the UK. 'Driven By You' won him his first solo Ivor Novello Award, for 'Best Theme From A TV/Radio Commercial'.

Back To The Light was released in the UK in September 1992 and February 1993 in the US. It peaked at Number 6 in the UK and Number 159 across the Atlantic. Aside from the aforementioned 'Driven By You', 'Too Much Love Will Kill You' peaked at Number 5 in the UK with 'Back To The Light' at Number 19 and 'Resurrection' at Number 33.

Critics were generous in their praise for the album.

The Advocate said: "While *Back To The Light* not surprisingly features plenty of guitar, May can't be accused of self-indulgence. Every track is a song in its own right, not simply an excuse for a solo. The exception is the album's sole instrumental, 'Last Horizon'. Even here, May doesn't sacrifice compositional integrity for shallow virtuoso display. On the lighter side, *Back To The Light* includes an affectionate spoof of country music, 'Let Your Heart Rule Your Head'. It's a foot-tapping number including clever country guitar-picking from May. Even without his late frontman, May is a vital artist."

Asked by Kirk Blows of *RCD Magazine* in 1992 if he saw himself as a frontman, May responded: "It's early days yet. I sung until I bled in the studio and it's for other people to judge whether I pulled it off or not, but I did some things I didn't think I could do in the beginning. But it's very different doing it on stage. I don't know if I have the expertise or the flair, or even the physical capabilities to deliver that stuff for two hours. I seem to suffer from colds half my life anyway, but there's only one day in three where I can sing that stuff on the album, so I'm still wrestling with that problem."

He toured to support the album.

An early version of the band featured the late Cozy Powell on drums, Mike Moran and Rick Wakeman on keyboards with Maggie Ryder, Miriam Stockley and Chris Thompson on backing vocals. They took part in the Guitar Legends festival in Seville, Spain in October 1991.

May spoke about the gig to David Mead of *Guitarist* magazine in 1992. "Fun. Really great fun. I had the opportunity to get all my favourite people together. What made it fun on the night was the fact that we knew what we were doing. We put enough rehearsal in to know we were going to be okay; it wasn't people just going up there and jamming."

He continued: "I was particularly keen on the idea that Joe Satriani should play with Steve Vai. This was a one-off and a chance to do something special. They both played on my stuff and we all played with Joe Walsh, which was a really great buzz, pounding out 'Rocky Mountain Way'..."

By the end of 1992 May had officially formed the Brian May Band with Cozy Powell on drums, Michael Casswell on guitar, Neil Murray on bass with Maggie Ryder, Miriam Stockley and Chris Thompson on backing vocals. They played just five dates together during a South American tour in November supporting The B-52's and Joe Cocker.

"I didn't have much belief for the first three solo gigs we did in Brazil; I was catastrophically nervous and discovered I didn't have the physical energy to maintain it," May confessed to Simon Bradley of *Guitarist* in 1998. "I was a pool of sweat and hopelessly out of breath."

They played a gig in Argentina where the Queen fanbase is enormous and the audience were ecstatic during the Queen numbers which fuelled May's energy. He felt a great bout of relief as the audience dug his voice and enjoyed the show. He forgot he was nervous because the reception was so powerful from the crowd and so from that moment on he felt he could handle the role of frontman. The shows got gradually better and better.

As with any frontman, May fed of the audiences' enthusiasm. It was a massive step moving from the guitarist of a band to the frontman but gradually May built up confidence and learned techniques on how to handle a crowd. Going on tour was great therapy for May.

However, as time progressed, May felt that the band

didn't gel sufficiently and so made some changes to the line-up with Jamie Moses replacing Michael Caswell and Catherine Porter and Shelley Preston replacing the three backing singers.

The latest version of the Brian May Band commenced a world tour on February 23, 1993 in support of Guns N' Roses in the US where they also performed some headlining shows of their own.

Reviewing the Austin Texas show on February 25, the *San Antonio Express* said: "Playing a half-dozen tracks off his new album, *Back To The Light*, May made only one musical nod to his former band when he worked the hard-rock guitar break in 'Bohemian Rhapsody' into an extended version of 'Resurrection', a track off the new album. And he seemed happy to be back on stage, greeting the crowd with 'It's nice to be back in the land of the living.'"

In Europe the band supported Valentine.

The UK tour dates ran as follows: Edinburgh Playhouse, June 4; Whitley Bay Ice Rink, June 5; Glasgow Barrowlands, June 6; Manchester Apollo, June 8; Sheffield City Hall, June 9; Cardiff Ice Rink, June 11; Birmingham NEC, June 12 and Brixton Academy, June 15.

May spoke to *GMTV* about the initial UK tour: "It's very, very different and I love it. It takes everything out of me. I mean with Queen I used to roll up in a city and go shopping and stuff and I'd arrive half an hour before the gig and I could change and go on, I was fine, I could do it every night of the week. With this it takes every ounce of mental and physical preparation to actually do it, because it's just so draining, I mean I know what Fred went through now, when you're singing, and of course I'm playing as well so I don't really get a moment off."

The band returned to the UK in October after shows in Europe, US and Japan. May was having trouble with his voice and so 'Driven By You' was dropped from the setlist in November.

The *Milwaukee Sentinel* reviewed May's gig in Milwaukee on October 14 and said: "Fortunately, May's style hasn't much changed. Wednesday's nearly SRO crowd at the Modjeska Theater was treated to an evening of new songs driven by May's stellar guitar with a few old favorites thrown into the mix. Opening the show with 'Back To The Light', May filled the theater with his powerful leads. Superlative fret work is to be expected from a professional of May's caliber. However, his vocals rarely emphasized during his Queen years proved to be a pleasant surprise. May seemed to approach his singing in the same manner he plays the guitar strong and clear."

A typical setlist ran as follows: 'The Dark', 'Back To The Light', 'Driven By You', 'Tie Your Mother Down', 'Love Token', 'Headlong', 'Love Of My Life' ''39' (intro), 'Let Your Heart Rule Your Head', 'Too Much Love Will Kill You', (Spike Edney keyboard solo), 'Since You've Been Gone', 'Now I'm Here', (Guitar Extravagance), 'Resurrection', (Coz Powell drum solo), '1812 Overture', 'Bohemian Rhapsody' (Reprise), 'Resurrection' (Reprise), (Band Introduction), 'Last Horizon', 'We Will Rock You', 'God (The Dream Is Over)' and 'Hammer To Fall'.

Having been on the road since for much of the year, the tour came to an end in Spain on December 18, 1993 and May's solo career was stalled after he returned to the studio with fellow Queen members, Roger Taylor and John Deacon to work on tracks that became the final album to feature Freddie Mercury, *Made In Heaven*.

"The others had already begun without me, so it started

off in a fairly stressful way, anyway," May said to Maura Sutton of *Classic Rock* in 1998. "Basically, I spent the next two years of my life either sitting in front of a computer trying to make the most of the scraps that we had of Freddie's vocal, or arranging and producing and performing to fill in all the gaps. It was an enormous project and it's so much easier if you've got all the guys in the band around you. We didn't have that situation, but the aim was to make an album that sounded like we did.'

He continued: "We were trying to make an album up to the same performance and arranging and producing standards of the others, and I think we succeeded. It's definitely a kind of fantasy album. It's like what if Queen had still existed, because there was no such thing at that point. It had its moments of great joy and discovery, but a lot of hard slog and a lot of hard bits emotionally."

As a momentum of the Brian May Band, *Live At Brixton Academy* was released in February 1994. It was recorded on June 15, 1993 at the famous London venue. A few edits were made, such as a keyboard solo before 'Last Horizon' which was extended because of technical issues with May's guitars.

The most disappointing omission of all was the lack of

a cover of John Lennon's 'God (The Dream Is Over)' with new lyrics. May had played it throughout the tour but had not received a response from Lennon's widow Yoko Ono as to whether he could use it or not, and so it could not be included.

The final version of the album features a number of Queen songs as well as some Brian May originals, and even a cover of Rainbow's 'Since You've Been Gone' (Cozy Powell was a member of Rainbow).

The setlist ran as follows: 'The Dark', 'Back To The Light', 'Driven By You', 'Tie Your Mother Down', 'Love Token', 'Headlong', 'Love Of My Life', ''39', 'Let Your Heart Rule Your Head', 'Too Much Love Will Kill You', 'Since You've Been Gone', 'Now I'm Here', 'Guitar Extravagance', 'Resurrection', 'Last Horizon', 'We Will Rock You' and 'Hammer To Fall'.

The album features in full the talents of Brian May on guitars and vocals, Cozy Powell on drums, Neil Murray on bass, Spike Edney on keyboards and vocals, Jamie Moses on guitars and vocals with backing singers Shelley Preston and Cathy Porter.

The album peaked at Number 20 in the UK but did not

get a US release. The dreadful album cover certainly doesn't do the music justice. Still, the opus is fondly thought of by fans and a fitting tribute to his band.

Reviewing the album on *All Music*, Geoff Orens writes: "However, even a live setting can't help the clunker 'Too Much Love Will Kill You'. The Queen tracks are a mixed bag. May just doesn't have the voice to tackle the harder-edged 'Headlong' and 'Tie Your Mother Down'. These tracks and a quite lifeless 'We Will Rock You' sorely miss Freddie Mercury's commanding vocals.

However, the medley of the old Queen track ''39' with May's 'Let Your Heart Rule Your Head' works quite well, in part because May sung the original version."

May's next album would see him rediscovering himself. He didn't want another introspective album but rather one that would see him revisit his roots, his influences.

"I went all the way around the world with the Brian May Band as it was then, and what we did was go straight back into the Queen area because we made the *Made In Heaven* album, and at the end of that – which was really two years of hard slog, and quite hard emotional business – I kinda didn't know who I was again." May admitted to *Talk Radio* in 1998.

However, it would be quite some time before May would return to the studio to make a second full length solo album and complete his solo career of the 1990s.

May enjoyed the freedom of a solo career, as he expressed to *Music Scene Magazine* in 1998. "I can do whatever I want. What I miss is the input and also sometimes also almost a bit the fights with the others. At recording sessions with Queen everything was hot, we all had tons of ideas, there was also some kind of competition and that was what made it so lively. I mean if Freddie would walk through this door right at this moment, I would instantly want to work with him again. The new situation is much more open to me, I don't have so much pressure anymore, not from the record company and not from the financial side or any kinds of deadlines. Now I get to experience other things, I get the chance to work with many other musicians, I get to do the score for a video game or to do a special for radio."

May was keen to distance himself from the Queen moniker when it came to his own projects and so in 1995 a single was released called 'The Amazing Spider-Man' and he also found time to record two songs ('Il Colosso' and 'What We Are Made Of' for the soundtrack to the 1996 movie, *The Adventures Of Pinocchio*. He also recorded two songs to two compilations: 'One Rainy Wish' for the Jimi Hendrix tribute, *In From The Storm* and 'F.B.I.' for the Hank Marvin and The Shadows tribute, *Twang!*.

May resumed his solo career in 1996 with a planned covers album called *Heroes*; also the name of David Bowie's 1977 opus. He decided, instead, to make it an album of new songs and renamed it *Another World*; opting for a personal approach to the album.

"Here I was back with the Queen hat on thinking, 'What on, what the hell was [*Back To The Light* and the tour] about?'" May said to *Talk Radio* in 1998. "So yes I plunged into doing, into revisiting the things which had made me tick in the very beginning. Like way before Queen, and started looking at all those things which I got excited about as a kid, like Buddy Holly and Little Richard and Elvis records, and all those guitarists who were on there, like Ricky Nelson records and stuff. And that was my little kind of my project for that moment; and I thought, yes, the album will probably come out as a load of covers."

May already had some original recordings at hand for the finishes release: 'On My Way Up' and 'Business' had both been penned back in 1993 for the TV show *Frank Stubbs Promotes*.

May spoke to Radio Clyde 1 in 1998 about the track, 'The Business': "Actually, more than that I think, quite a while ago. Yes, I did some fragments. This song, I common with a lot of other tracks on my whole album, was initially inspired from the outside. I got all these little kind of commissions and triggers and inspirations from outside, and this was a TV thing, yes.

They asked me to write song about this guy who basically gets up every morning and tries his best and always tried new angles, but he never quite makes it, he's like the eternal optimist but the eternal loser. So, I wrote them some fragments which they used for the TV series, and then I started to realise that I was writing about myself, you know, as always is the case. You're always drawing on something inside yourself, and so I developed the song and worked on it and it eventually became this thing called 'The Business'. It features Cozy very heavily, as you probably can tell."

May had plenty of material in his archives for an album. A huge fan of science-fiction writer Isaac Asimov and robots, 'Cyborg' had been written for the computer game *Rise 2: Resurrection* while the title-track itself was written for May's friend, the screenwriter and director Peter Howitt, for the British film *Sliding Doors* but it was not included on the final soundtrack.

"I decided to interact with different people because I thought it would be very good for me," May admitted to *Guitarist*'s Simon Bradley in 1998 about the album and exploring new musical horizons with other artists. "Previously I'd just there like a hermit, working on *Made In Heaven*, and I suppose it has a certain intensity because of that. But I felt it was time to start to let stuff in from the outside. So not only did I go out and guest with people, I also made sure that I answered the phone. I had a lot of people ringing me up asking me if I could do this or do that, and I did them all."

However, despite scraping the idea of a covers album, three covers were included on the final album: 'One Rainy Wish', Larry William's 'Slow Down' and Mott The Hoople's 'All The Way From Memphis'

The Mott cover came about after former Mott keyboardist Morgan Fisher – who also played keyboards for Queen on tour in 1982 – asked May to record a cover for a planned tribute album. "Mott The Hoople was really our [Queen's] first experience of life on the road, and a pretty blinding experience it was, I must say," May said to *Radio Clyde 1* in 1998. "It's always remained close to my heart, cos we grew up on that tour, we had to, it was just insanity, and to survive you had to adapt, you had to become a rock 'n' roll kind of animal and in the good sense of the word, you know. And, yeah, it was phenomenal. And I used to watch them do 'All The Way From Memphis' every night, and every night the place would erupt, it was like an earthquake. They really were a fantastic band live. Should have stayed together, I have to say. 'Young Dudes' was a big one, but Mr Bowie wrote that, but for me 'Memphis' is the one, and I always wanted to do this song."

He had also recorded 'F.B.I', 'Hot Patootie' from *The Rocky Horror Picture Show* (Anita Dobson was in the NSO Ensemble cast of *The Rocky Horror Show* and May recorded it for the soundtrack album), 'Only Make Believe' by Conway Twitty and Buddy Holly's 'Maybe Baby'. He also recorded a version of Elvis Presley's 'Marie's The Name ('His Latest Flame')', which was originally by Del Shannon. A rough demo of May's version was leaked without his approval.

May spoke about the album to *Guitarist*'s Simon Bradley: "Now, when someone asks me to write a song about, say, a robot, I go away and do it. From that, I get more inspiration, which becomes another track. When I was writing the album, all these bits came together and I realised what I was trying to do."

The album features musicians Spike Edney, Ken Taylor, Cozy Powell, Neil Murray and Jamie Moses.

"I got all the boys in to play this, this is the one track on the album which really was live," May said to *Radio Clyde 1* in 1998: "Cozy Powell, Neil Murray, Spike Edney, who was the guy who was normally playing keyboards round the back of the stage for Queen, and Jamie Moses who has become a very good friend, and support guitarist. We all came in and we just played loads of songs, stuff that we knew. You know, we all know 'Slow Down', we all know 'Maybe Baby', we all know 'It's Only Make Believe'. We did a load of stuff just for fun really, and to have some stuff on tape and I'm so glad that we did it now, because Cozy [is] no longer here, it has a new kind of significance for me. I've been getting the tapes out, just today as a matter of fact, and we've been mixing a couple, and at some point, I think, we will put out a little EP of our own, a little rock and roll, kind of retro rock EP, which I'm really excited about now."

'Slow Down' was the only track they recorded live. Picking a Mott The Hoople track to cover was in some ways a no brainer for May considering the band's significant in British rock 'n' roll history and their closeness to Queen.

"They influenced Queen very much," May said to *Guitar & Bass* in 1998. "We were on tour with them, and this was our first experience towards that. We learned from them what it means to be on stage. They kept contact to the audience which was pretty unusual at that time. Most people just stood on the stage, played for themselves and took a nap. And if the music was over the audience was happy. But Mott The Hoople were different, they gave everything on stage and in my opinion they were a wonderful rock 'n' roll band. They understood everything: The necessity to communicate, the sounds, the visual side; they knew that you need a fix form for a good show. We were prepared in theory at that time, they went into praxis. That song of them we recorded like a live track."

Other musicians that contributed to the opus included London Metropolitan Orchestra (strings on 'One Rainy Wish', conducted by Michael Kamen), Cathy Porter (backing vocals on 'On My Way Up'), Shelley Preston (backing vocals on 'On My Way Up' and 'All The Way From Memphis'), Nikki Love (backing vocals on 'All The Way From Memphis'), Becci Glover (backing vocals on 'All The Way From Memphis'), Taylor Hawkins (drums on 'Cyborg'), Jeff Beck (guitar on 'The Guv'nor') and Ian Hunter (guest raconteur on 'All The Way From Memphis').

Speaking about his collaboration with Jeff Beck on 'The Guv'nor' May said to *Radio Clyde I* in 1998: "I can't play like that, good grief! There's only one person who can play like Jeff Beck, and that's 'The Guv'nor'! Yeah! Yeah, I was very, very chuffed, and I was very honoured that he played on my record. He's been a hero of mine since I started, and I'm happy to say that he's a friend now. I'm always a little bit in awe, though, I mean, like, he is the guitarist's guitarist and he's scary guy. And the song…this song was actually written about a fighter in the beginning because there was a film due to come out, called 'The Guv'nor'. It may still come out, I don't know, but I think they ran out of money temporarily. But it's about a fist fighter, a bare knuckle fighter, and I wrote a song about that, which was quite a serious song in the beginning, but I began to see a little metaphor there, and a slightly amusing side, cos I thought, Well, to us guys, who think we can play guitar, Jeff Beck is 'The Guv'nor'. So I wrote it about him, and he played on it. He did a fantastic job."

The album's tracklisting features twelve songs: 'Space', 'Business', 'China Belle', 'Why Don't We Try Again?', 'On My Way Up', 'Cyborg', 'The Guv'nor', 'Wilderness', 'Slow Down', 'One Rainy Wish', 'All The Way From Memphis' and 'Another World'.

"Yes, there is a theme to it I guess," May explained to *BBC Radio 2* in 1998. "It's a long story, but the story stretches over six years since the last proper solo album that I made. In between, there was making the *Made In Heaven* album, the final Queen album, and many, many other projects. I got involved in all kinds of things this last few years and really enjoyed it – found it very stimulating working, you know, with film directors and TV producers and stuff but, of course, the centre of it all is playing live, and I think my, my trigger, my stimulus for getting this thing finished in the end was that I could get back out on tour and do it. But yes, there's a lot of my life in this album as it has been, it's not just autobiography, biography, it's not just that, but it's everything is triggered by what you see. You know, if you're an artist you sit there with your (sharp intake of breath) with your clean canvass and you paint what you see to an extent, tempered by what's in your brain, and it's the same for a musician, I think."

Tragically, Powell was killed in a car accident on April 5, 1998 on the M4 Motorway near Bristol. There was an upcoming tour planned and so a new drummer had to be sought out very quickly.

"He was something wonderful, really a legend and something of a hero to me," May said to Poland's *Radio 3* in 1998. "He became a very close friend. If he walked into a room he would bring the spirit of the whole place up always and suddenly everything seems like it's fun again. A great personality and somebody wonderful being direct with. I could always throw any suggestions and he said 'yes, yes...I'm gonna try it'. With a lot of musicians it's difficult to do that, you know? Cozy was always open and always positive."

Steve Ferrone was hired to finish off recording the drums and joined the band on stage for five showcase and acoustic presentation dates in Europe before the world tour commenced which featured former Alice Cooper and current KISS drummer Eric Singer. Ferrone moved on to working with Tom Petty. The band was built around Powell and after listening to the album again May felt that Powell would want him to go out on tour with the album. Singer was phenomenal with the dangerous energy of Foo Fighters Taylor Hawkins.

"Eric was recommended to me by my friend Tony Iommi of Black Sabbath who rang me when he heard the news," May said to the *Birmingham Mail* in 1998. "We had to decide whether to get a new drummer or cancel the tour. Cozy's death was a hard knock – it still is – but when I heard Eric play it blew me away. He's incredibly explosive and technically brilliant."

May has always had strong ideas of where a song should go – it isn't just about the guitar sound or the voice. There's the melody then the voice, the arrangement, the guitar and the production. Of course there are lyrics too. A strong voice should unite all those elements. May has his own sound, a unique riff and arrangement that has become his trademark.

"…you know most people have said, that the voice sounds really strong on this album and that really was my priority," May said to *Talk Radio* in 1998. "Because, to be truthful, even with Queen, you know, I had the same feelings about what I do now. Number one is the song, if you don't have a decent song – forget it. Number two is the singer, because if you don't have a decent singer to put across the song – again, forget it. You can play the greatest guitar solo in the world and it doesn't mean a thing. And after those two things you get into the production and the guitar and everything, but I was determined that the voice would be something that would get across the necessary feeling and passion and whatever."

The album spawned two singles releases: 'Business' (which has since been renamed 'The Business') was released in June 1998 and peaked at Number 51 while 'Why Don't We Try Again?' was released in September and peaked at Number 44.

Having experience some personal difficulties over the past several years, May found solace in his work. Working on *Another World* proved to be a therapeutic experience.

"While I was recording this album, I was fighting on several battles at one time," May said to *Best Magazine* in 1998. "I was looking for the possible directions I could orientate my life to, and this idea (expressed in the song quoted above) comes from a friend, who offers a previously unreleased kind of therapy. These are little tricks that work with mind but nothing to do with a classical therapy, with which you have to go through your past again, back to childhood. It's an exceptional work on the brain little mental blocks. You just go backward a little and you try to spot the triggers that don't work. I was not going well at all, and he taught me how to create this space around me. For instance, if a pain related to your past obsesses you, you learn to 'setup' this space between you and the past. It lets you be a bit stiller, to suffer less for the next five minutes, hours and sometimes days that follow. It also works physically."

One of his favourite songs is the title-track as he felt that people could relate to it. It sums up the way a lot of people feel. You get an idea, it collapses and then you hope for something better.

"I am fairly protective of being an ordinary person if you know what I mean," May admitted to Paul Cashmere of

Undercover in 1998. "That matters a lot to me. I have kids and I need to live a fairly ordinary life. It is important for me to be able to step out of the sort of rock and roll world and be a person. The thing that you are talking about, the beginning of the album which is called 'Space' comes from a friend of mine who does linguistic programming. It sounds like something to do with a computer but it is actually alternative psychotherapy. It is based on very simple experimental principals and what they do is they reprogram your mind so that you are not scared of things. It's like any problem that you have is in your mind so they will re-program your mind so that it doesn't perceive it in the same way. It's a technique that works pretty well. This space thing is one of them. If something is hurting you, you put an imaginary clearing around yourself, until you have enough space to breathe and then you get on with your life."

Critics were (mostly) enthusiastic over the album.

Simon Bradley of *Guitarist Magazine* wrote: "If it's the trademark guitar orchestrations you're after, the opening salvo of 'Business' and 'China Belle', the latter's structure and lyrics having more to do with Bryan Adams than anyone else, should slake your thirst for a while. Like all the best Queen albums,

Brian's made sure that there's something here for just about everyone."

Metal Hammer's Jerry Ewing wrote: "Although it won't surprise anyone who's revelled in the likes of 'Brighton Rock' or 'Now I'm Here', the monolithic riffing that spurs on 'Business' or the lyrically suspect 'China Belle' confirm that May can still pack a rock punch that would do Lennox Lewis proud. Both are gargantuan slices of pounding hard rock that prove there's life in the old boy yet."

Peter Kane of *Q Magazine* was less enthused with a two star review: "Some artless piano ballads, a host of undignified rockers marooned in the darkest recess of the '70s as well as aimless whacks at Mott The Hoople's beloved 'All The Way From Memphis' and Larry Williams' distinctly creaky 'Slow Down' sound like a poor return for 3 years of studio graft. Let's hope he enjoyed making it because there's bugger all pleasure to be had at this end of things."

Meanwhile, *Total Guitar* said: "Think of all the best 'Brian May' bits in Queen's album repertoire – the rock section of 'Now I'm Here', the beautiful rock solos from 'Killer Queen' and of course 'Bo Rhap'; plus the layered guitar orchestras on just about everything. Combine these with some BIG harmonies and quirky bits of songwriting (one track sung by a robot, another a eulogy to Jeff Beck) and add a few possibly ill-advised covers ('All The Way From Memphis', 'Slow Down'), then file the whole lot under 'interesting'."

NME wrote: "Bonzoid drum splashes from the late Cozy Powell bludgeon home the unfettered pneumatic power of 'Business', but it's on the covers herein that May truly allows the hammer to fall: Hendrix's 'One Rainy Wish' is a multi-layered swoon, while Mott The Hoople's 'All The Way From Memphis' is sheer unfettered adrenalin. Sure he'll never boast the immeasurable vocal power of Fred, yet as someone once said, the Queen is dead. So cry havoc, and let rip the clogs of roar!"

How did May cope with Queen's lasting legacy? It would invariably overshadow his solo work. After all, who's interested in Mick Jagger's solo projects? Even Freddie Mercury's solo career didn't set the world on fire.

"Queen does cast a very long shadow, but I apply the same quality standards to my solo records as I did to Queen – which is probably why it takes so damn long," May said to *Q*

Magazine's Mark Blake in 1998. "It's been six years since the last one (*Back To The Light*) and I like to think that since then I've got out in the real world and interacted with people a bit more, which has to be a good thing."

The Brian May Band hit the road for some dates including a full length UK tour but not before he joined Steve Vai and Joe Satriani on stage when the G3 tour rolled into London to play the Shepherd's Bush Empire on Wednesday 4 June. He then flew to Italy and France before returning to London for some promotional concerts.

The *Another World* tour started in Spain in September and took to parts all over Europe before returning home to Old Blighty. The UK tour dates ran as follows: Nottingham Royal Concert Hall, October 24; London Royal Albert Hall, October 25; Bristol Colston Hall, October 27; Birmingham Academy, October 28; Newcastle City Hall, October 30; Manchester Apollo, October 31; Sheffield City Hall, November 2 and Glasgow Royal Concert Hall, November 3.

Kerrang!'s Steve Beebee wrote of the Birmingham NIA show: "The 51-year-old guitarist is just as interested in astronomy as he is in rock music, and he's therefore not the most compelling of frontmen. But Mercury was a showman who will never be replaced – May knows that, and so do his fans. 'Another World' and 'Driven By You' are inevitable, but they're not the reason anyone here has shelled out #17.50. This was simply an interesting evening out for those who remember Queen with fondness."

A typical setlist of the tour ran like this: 'Dance With The Devil', 'Only Make Believe', 'C'mon Babe', 'Space' 'Since You've Been Gone', 'Business', (Spike Edney keyboard solo), 'China Belle', 'White Man' (Intro), 'Fat Bottomed Girls', 'I Want It All', 'Headlong', 'Tear It Up', 'The Show Must Go On', (Neil Murray bass solo), 'Last Horizon', 'Love Of My Life', 'Driven By You', (band introduction), 'On My Way Up', 'Hammer To Fall', (guitar solo), 'Resurrection', (Eric Singer drum solo), 'We Will Rock You', 'Tie Your Mother Down', 'Another World', 'All The Way From Memphis' and 'No-One But You (Only The Good Die Young)'.

He played Russia, Japan and Australia in November, with the last night of the tour in Brisbane on November 28.

The Advertiser wrote of the Adelaide show on November 25: "At the same time, May asserted his own musicianship and personality as a late-blooming frontman. It's an amazing legacy to confront and May did it with good humor and humility, embracing the rowdy reception. His virtuosity on guitar remained something to behold, especially at close range, as he wove intricate patterns using a series of delay pedals."

May felt his solo career had come to an end. Apart from *Furia*, a soundtrack recorded the year after, May has not released a solo album leaving *Another World* as his last word. May has since concentrated on a number of other projects. It seems unlikely at this stage that a third album will ever emerge.

Asked by *Best Magazine* in 1998 how he has evolved in life as a musician and a man, he responded: "I think we get older more in what fills our mind than on the level of the age. You have to begin to deal with the death of your parents, of your friends. These are the things that can make you change the perception of the speed life is going. As a musician I think I am better than I used to be, not necessarily technically, but in my ability of having more outlook in my playing. I've been incredibly impatient for long and I stuck too much to every note I played."

Alas, the Brian May Band was put to rest.

May had kept himself busy since the turn of the century, however. There have been various projects both Queen and non-Queen related.

May has often been confused with the Australian composer of the same name who was responsible for the soundtracks to films *Mad Max* and *Dr. Giggies*, but in fact, that Brian May died in April 1997 and Queen guitarist Brian May has only ever composed one entire soundtrack. The Queen guitarist has forever been asked about the *Mad Max* soundtrack.

Released in November 2000 and recorded at CTS and Allerton Hill Studios in Wembley between January and March 1999 (though May spent time living in Paris in January), *Furia* is the soundtrack to the 1999 French film. May was approached by the French filmmaker Alexandra Aja, director of the 1997 indie film *Over The Rainbow*, after he concluded his *Another World* tour in November 1998 to compose some music for his next film after the guitarist's name was mentioned by a friend. May saw a rough cut of the film and was so taken aback by it that he offered to compose the entire soundtrack, a first for him (though Queen had recorded music for *Flash Gordon* and *Highlander*). Aja co-wrote the film with Grégory Levasseur, adapted from the science fiction short story 'Graffiti' by Julio Cortázar. The only song on the most instrumental soundtrack to feature lyrics is 'Dream Of Thee'. Written, produced and arranged by May, the album features The London Musician's Orchestra conducted by Michael Reed with Dave Lee on solo horn, Phillipa Davies on flute, Rolf Wilson on first violin and Emily May on ('Apparition') vocal.

May spoke to Darren Davis of *Launch* in 2001 about his then current projects: "…it's something that I'm very proud of. It's the first full soundtrack that I've done. You know, I've done loads of bits and pieces for films, including *Highlander*, and *Flash*, and all those things, but this was a complete soundtrack. I do a lot of stuff. I've done a lot of blues recently, for some strange reason. I was beginning to have this feeling that I'd like go get back to blues, and I've been playing it with a number of people. That will probably see the light of day – not as a solo album, but as a couple of projects. The big thing at the moment – it's going to sound strange, but it's in essence not to do with music directly, because I'm acting as a producer – we're putting together a film, me and my friend, about a subject that I've been passionate about for a very long time. I'm not going to tell you what it is right now, but it's a kind of historical film, and it's about putting the record straight in history as best we can and as honestly as we can. It's a long-term project. I've been on it for about a year, and we have a few appointments with studios. That's been my biggest passion at the moment."

The rest of May's projects included bits and pieces with various artists and two reunions with Queen.

On October 22, 2000 he joined Motörhead onstage at Brixton Academy with former Motörhead guitarist "Fast" Eddie Clarke for a rousing version of 'Overkill'. It was the band's 25th Anniversary show. May also made a special appeared at the Genesis reunion gig at Twickenham Stadium in 2007. He is friends with Phil Collins.

May then contributed a guitar solo to Meat Loaf's album, *Hang Cool, Teddy Bear*. May had previously contributed a guitar solo to the track 'Bad For Good', featuring on 2006's *Bat Out Of Hell III: The Monster Is Loose*.

Throughout the 2010s, May had continued to make guest appearances on other artists work by contributing guitar to the Lady Gaga song 'You And I' which features on her 2011 album *Born This Way*. In June of the same year he performed with Tangerine Dream at Tenerife's Starmus Festival, which celebrated the 50th Anniversary of Yuri Gagarin's first spaceflight.

In August 2011 he took the stage to jam with the US metal band My Chemical Romance for electrifying versions of 'We Will Rock You' and 'Welcome To The Black Parade' at the Reading Festival and two days later on August 28 he performed 'You And I' with Lady Gaga at the 2011 MTV Video Music Awards at LA's Nokia Theatre. He flew back to the UK to join The Darkness onstage at Hammersmith Apollo in London for three songs including 'Tie Your Mother Down'.

In 2011he performed in N-Dubz's frontman's Dappy solo single 'Rockstar' and later performed 'We Will Rock You' together for BBC Radio One's Live Lounge.

On August 12, 2012 May played part of 'Brighton Rock' at the closing ceremony for the 2012 Summer Olympics in London; he was later soon by Roger Taylor and Jessie J for a performance of 'We Will Rock You'.

On September 16, 2012 May joined a host of rock stars (Led Zeppelin bassist John Paul Jones, Ian Paice of Deep Purple and singers Bruce Dickinson of Iron Maiden and Alice Cooper at the Sunflower Jam charity concert at London's Royal Albert Hall.

In 2014 May even found time to record the soundtrack for a little British indie film called *51 Degrees* which premiered at the 2014 Starmus Festival. The film was directed by the German filmmaker Grigorij Richters.

May had struck up a professional relationship with singer and theatre actress Kerry Ellis ever since she was cast (after a reported seven auditions) as Meat in the Queen musical *We Will Rock You*, written by Ben Elton and produced by Robert De Niro. She sang the 'No-One But You (Only The Good Die Young)'.

"I really wrote it about Freddie," Brian told ITV talk show *This Morning* in 1997 about'No-One But You (Only The Good Die Young)'. "It goes back to Jimi Hendrix, and in a way that's what the song's about. It's like maybe you die young, but you burn, you know. A lot of people go for it, and the metaphor is that they fly too close to the sun, which is like the Icarus legend. Icarus flew too high and his wings fell off, his wax melted and he fell in the sea."

May had first met her back in 2002 after she had

performed as Martine McCutcheon's understudy in the 2001 play *My Fair Lady*. Ellis would go on to star in such West End and national musicals as *Les Miserables*, *Wicked* and *Oliver*, *Miss Saigon*, *Chess*, *RENT* and *The War Of The Worlds*.

"I was just bowled over by her, right from when she came to audition for the part of Meat all those years ago [alarmingly, *We Will Rock You* is still going strong at the Dominion Theatre after eight years]," he admitted to Rachel Cooke of *The Guardian* in 2012. "I'm just a fan, I suppose. She has the most stunning instrument, and a passion that you always look for in singers but so rarely find."

The EP *Wicked In Rock* was arranged and produced by May and Steve Sidwell. May also played guitar on the songs and brought in his Foo Fighters buddy Taylor Hawkins on drums. The EP consists of new orchestrations of 'Defying Gravity' and 'I'm Not That Girl' from *Wicked* and the Queen song 'No-One But You (Only The Good Die Young)'.

May continued to collaborate with Kerry Ellis when he accompanied during the encore for four shows in June 2009.

May produced and arranged her debut solo album in 2010, called *Anthems*, recorded at Abbey Road Studios with a 70 piece orchestra, which peaked at Number 15 in the UK.

Baz Bamigboye of the *Daily Mail* wrote a positive review: "This quiet, calm singer has a voice that raises the roof of whatever theatre she performs in, but she does not belt. Instead, she's able to mould her soprano into a rock vibe that gives a lift to whatever song comes her way."

The *Independent* said: "Now her debut album *Anthems* from Decca is writ even larger with an intoxicating mix of show and rock anthems giving full rein to Kerry's laser belt and May's impassioned and fabulously distinctive guitar sound. The arrangements are big, the songs bigger with show-stoppers (from *Wicked* and *Chess And Kristina*) rubbing shoulders with some May/Queen classics. May has gone on record as saying that Kerry's voice is proving as powerful an inspiration for him as Freddie Mercury's. That's some compliment."

Leading up to the release of the album the pair performed at the BBC's *Proms In The Park* event with a setlist of songs from *Anthems* as well as a medley of Queen songs. They also performed at The Royal British Legion's *Festival Of Remembrance* at the Royal Albert Hall; the British Royal Family, including Queen Elizabeth II, were in attendance. Ellis and May promoted the album by appearing on a number of high profile British shows such as *Tonight's The Night*, *The Michael Ball Show*, *This Morning* and *The Alan Titchmarsh Show*. They also performed live at the BBC Radio Theatre and the London nightclub, G-A-Y.

A big step forward was when he joined Ellis on tour for 16 dates across the UK in May 2011. It was called *Anthems: The Tour* and after a charity concert at the Royal Albert Hall on May 1, the tour began proper May 23 and ended on July 16 with a special titled Anthems in the Park at RAF Cranwell.

Their band was dubbed the Anthems Ensemble and consisted of Stuart Morley on keyboards, Jeff Leach on keyboards, Jamie Humphries on guitar, Neil Fairclough on bass, Rufus Taylor on drums, Kirstie Roberts and Niamh McNally on backing vocals.

Ellis spoke to *The Public Reviews* in 2011 about working with May: "He's been really great to me right from the start really, he's been a champion of mine. He's supported everything I've done, other shows, and then obviously he supported me working on my first album. I think we share a passion for the music, and Queen were very theatrical in their time, so I think it would have happened for them at some point anyway, if Freddie was still here; I think they would have gone on to celebrate musical theatre as well."

A typical setlist ran as follows: 'Overture', 'Dangerland', 'I Am Not That Girl', 'I Can't Be Your Friend', 'Diamonds Are Forever', 'Somebody To Love', 'Last Horizon', 'Love Of My Life', 'I Loved A Butterfly', 'Save Me', 'No On But You (Only The Good Die Young)', 'You Have To Be There', 'I Love It When You Call', 'Defying Gravity', 'We Will Rock You', 'We Are The Champions', 'Anthem' and 'Tie Your Mother Down'.

"At the moment 'cause we're on tour and we're very involved with the show and what we're doing together, to perform 'Tie Your Mother Down' at the end of the show is very uplifting for me personally because it summarizes the show at the moment," Ellis explained to *Rock Cellar*'s Ken Sharp in 2014. "It's great fun. It's a different twist on how the song is usually played and that's really uplifting for me personally."

As with the album, the tour received mostly positive reviews.

The Scotsman said of the Festival Theatre performance:

"*Anthems* treads a fine line between wonderfully overblown fun and high-gloss hotel karaoke; the former exhibited on the brooding bombast of 'Dangerland', and the latter illustrated by an insipid rendition of 'Diamonds Are Forever'. It's ironic that the evening's best moments are delivered by May himself. An acoustic version of 'Love Of My Life', which he dedicates to his mother, is done simply and executed beautifully, while the extended guitar solo beforehand is superlative."

Craig Hepworth of *What's On Stage* noted: "When Ellis sings and sings from the heart (and songs from her debut album) it's a real treat, but with so many Queen songs thrown in, it runs the risk of becoming a Queen tribute concert at times. Don't get me wrong, the music of Queen is wonderful and when Ellis sings songs like 'Somebody To Love' – it takes a few moments to get your breath back from the sheer power you have just seen on stage."

They changed the setlist all together for the 2012 UK tour dates (under the headline The Born Free Tour) in November: 'Born Free', 'I Loved A Butterfly', 'I (Who Have Nothing)', 'Dust In The Wind', 'The Kissing Me Song', 'Somebody To Love', 'Nothing Really Has Changed', 'Life Is

Real', 'The Way We Were', 'Since You've Been Gone', ''39',
'Something', 'Love Of My Life', 'I'm Not That Girl', 'No-One
But You (Only The Good Die Young)', 'Last Horizon', 'Tie
Your Mother Down', 'Can't Be Your Friend', 'Knockin' On
Heaven's Door', 'We Will Rock You', 'We Are The
Champions', 'In The Bleak Midwinter', 'Born Free' and 'Crazy
Little Thing Called Love'.

Said Brian May in a press release as quoted on *Planet
Rock*: "Over the last year, Kerry and I have been recording new
material when our schedules have allowed it. As on the *Anthems*
album, some of the tracks have very big and splendid
arrangements, but we have become more and more fascinated
with the magic of great songs stripped down to their core and re-
interpreted in an 'acoustic' way. We find there is a purity which
makes the songs speak very clearly. Kerry's instincts as an
interpreter of songs are always inspiring, and the art of arranging
has always been one of my obsessions. We have found that the
two of us just working live off each other can distill the very
essence of a song – and that's what we hope to bring you in
these dates. After all, if you have great songs and a great singer,
what more do you need? Well, maybe just a little bit of guitar!"

The tour, which consisted of 11 dates around the Home Counties of England, began on November 5 2012 at the Apex in Bury St Edmunds, and finished on November 19 at the Swan Theatre in High Wycombe. Whereas Anthems: The Tour was a higher scaled production, The Born Free Tour was completely scaled down and acoustic with a candlelit stage.

Speaking to Aida Edemariam of *The Guardian* in 2012, May said: "It's almost like a reaction to the music that made Queen famous, though if you look at it some of it's very simple. 'We Will Rock You' is very simple. 'Millionaire Waltz' is highly complex."

They later played a free thirty minute acoustic set, which included Queen's 'Crazy Little Thing Called Love' at St Pancras railway station in London on March 1, 2013. The gig was to launch Tiger Track, a three week long tiger conservation event.

"One of the things that I love about Kerry is she does not do ornamentation for its own sake," May told Ken Sharp of *Rock Cellar* in 2014. "She sings from her heart. She speaks about singing the song as it was written and that's what I try to do as well. We love it and the audiences connect with it, no doubt."

In June and July of 2013 they played the UK and Europe continuing The Born Free Tour and comprising of three legs. The third and final leg, which consisted of seven shows on mainland Europe, was completed in Monteux, Switzerland on July 19.

Ann Clarkson of *The Shropshire Star* wrote of the Birmingham Town Hall show in June 2013: "The tour has been recorded for a new album, *Acoustic By Candlelight*, but as this was Birmingham it was acoustic by slightly naff electric candle effect lights – the city council doesn't allow candles in its fabulously restored historic town hall. But although it says acoustic, this is Brian May – so the Red Special was brought out for the signature solo, plus a few more tracks. Is this the only guitar that gets its own round of applause? The highlight for me was 'No-One But You', the song the three surviving members of Queen wrote in tribute to Freddie Mercury and which Kerry has made her own since she first sang it at the Dominion Theatre in 'We Will Rock You'."

Chris High of *Click Liverpool* reviewed the Liverpool Philharmonic show and enthused: "This was no Queen tribute act though – indeed the biggest surprise lay omission of 'Love Of My Life' – and the singer and musicians displayed such a finely tuned chemistry it was, at times, mesmeric to provide a truly fantastic night of music and song, in aid of a truly fantastic charity in the Born Free Foundation that had everybody posing and miming riffs along Lime Street well into the night."

May and Ellis released *Acoustic By Candlelight* on June 17, 2013 to coincide with the second leg of the tour. Consisting of fifteen songs, many of which were recorded during the 2012 tour, it picked up some good reviews. The album features 'Born Free', 'I Loved A Butterfly', 'I (Who Have Nothing)', 'Dust In The Wind', 'The Kissing Me Song', 'Nothing Really Has Changed', 'Life Is Real', 'The Way We Were', 'Something', 'Love Of My Life', 'I'm Not That Girl', 'I Can't Be Your Friend', 'In The Bleak Midwinter', 'Crazy Little Thing Called Love' and 'No-One But You (Only The Good Die Young)'.

Classic Rock Revisited's Jeb Wright said of the collection: "There is a cutesy original song called 'Kissing Me' which, again for this type of project works well. 'Born Free' is performed, as is 'The Way We Were'. Brian and Kerry pull out some Queen tunes, some deep cuts and some classics. As it turns out the 'new' versions of these classics are quite good and, along with 'Dust In The Wind', are the best in show. 'Life Is Real' is poignant in this setting, while 'We Will Rock You' and 'Crazy Thing Called Love' rock in their own way. ''39' comes across very well. One of the best received moments is 'Somebody To Love', a great song no matter what the version."

Dave White of *About.com: Classic Rock* enthused: "The bottom line is that this album brings together two consummate professionals who are talented artists, who are comfortable with a variety of musical styles, and who have the kind of natural chemistry that produces a pairing that just feels right on all counts. The chemistry is apparent on the CD, but even more so on the DVD where you can see as well as hear the interaction of the artists with one another, and with the audience. Thankfully, you don't have to choose one or the other."

Reviewing the accompanying DVD for *Get Ready To Rock*, Jason Ritchie wrote: "The CD collects a similar setlist to the DVD but recorded around the various venues that made up their UK tour in 2012. The CD also features four songs not available anywhere else including 'I Loved A Butterfly' a new song written by Brian May and 'I Can't Be Your Friend', which

May co-write with famed lyricist Don Black.

Queen fans will want this for the previously unavailable songs and as a memento for those lucky enough to see the band live. Plus this has a wider appeal as the Queen songs will be known to many and anyone who enjoys acoustic based music with a very powerful female vocal will be in seventh heaven with this DVD and CD."

Ellis also provided vocals for the 2013 May song 'The Badger Swagger', which supported Team Badger; a coalition of organisations that fight the planned cull of badgers in the UK.

"We're both very passionate about what we do and I think that's the basis of it," Ellis said to *The Public Reviews* in 2011 about her collaboration with May. "It's the passion of Brian with the guitar and me with singing, and that we just so enjoy performing. We also have great people to work with, which is always a bonus."

They resumed touring again in early 2014.

The 2014 setlist looked like this: 'I (Who Have Nothing)', 'I Loved A Butterfly', 'Dust In The Wind', 'Born Free', 'Somebody To Love', 'Tell Me What You See', 'Nothing Really Has Changed', 'The Way We Were', 'Something', 'So

Sad', ''39', 'The Kissing Me Song', 'I'm Not That Girl', 'If I Loved You', 'Last Horizon', 'Is This The World We Created?', 'Tie Your Mother Down', 'No-One But You (Only The Good Die Young)', 'We Will Rock You' and 'Crazy Little Thing Called Love'.

Speaking about future projects together, Ellis spoke to Andrew Clarke of *EADT24* in mid-2014: "We are planning to be in the studio at the end of June and into the beginning of July. Because we only have a set amount of money we have to be very disciplined and go into the studio, get it down and get out. When I have worked with Brian in the past, he has the luxury of having his own recording studio, so time was never an issue. But I think we will be all right because we know the material, the arrangements have all been worked out, so it should be fine."

Despite his enormous success in the music industry, though, he craves to be best known for his animal rights activism as he said to Aida Edemariam of *The Guardian* in 2012: "Yep. I won't be remembered in 1,000 years anyway, but I would like to leave this planet knowing that I did what I could to make it a better place, a more decent place, a more compassionate place."

Considering the success of the May-Ellis musical

partnership there's no question that it will continue for some time. But with Queen rejuvenated May's side projects will perhaps be put on the back burner for a while. Perhaps, one day there'll be a complete solo studio album. We live in hope.

Tour dates were shelved in late 2016 after May had to undergo hospital treatment.

More high-profile than both May and Taylor's career is that of Queen and Mercury's lasting legacy.

PHOTO BY ANDY BRAILSFORD

PHOTO BY ANDY BRAILSFORD

PHOTO BY ANDY BRAILSFORD

PHOTO BY ANDY BRAILSFORD

PHOTO BY ANDY BRAILSFORD

PHOTO BY ANDY BRAILSFORD

PHOTOS BY ANDY BRAILSFORD

QUEEN + PAUL RODGERS

"Roger has always been the one who's been keen to get back out on tour," May explained to Geoff Barton of *Classic Rock* in 2005 "It was me who was holding things back, because I didn't think things felt right. There was no one on the horizon who I thought could do the job of singing with us. And then suddenly we're looking at this man [Rodgers], who can not only do the job, he can do a lot more besides – he brings something completely new to it, and that's what turned me around."

Fans were bemused, excited and nervous when it was announced that Queen – that is Brian May and Roger Taylor – were planning to partner-up with blues singer Paul Rodgers of Free and Bad Company fame. Rodgers is one of Britain's greatest white blues singers but not a rock singer in the sense of Freddie Mercury of Steven Tyler. John Deacon chose not to come out of retirement. Was he asked to join?

The formation of this collaboration went back to 2004 with a benefit concert called Fender Strat Park which featured May and Rodgers performing a rendition of Free's 'All Right Now'. May and Rodgers had performed together onstage several times before, but this time they spoke of a collaboration. Roger Taylor joined and thus it became Queen + Paul Rodgers.

Queen were inducted into the UK Music Hall Of Fame in 2004, which marked the first live appearance of Queen + Paul Rodgers.

2004 also saw the release of *Queen On Fire – Live At The Bowl*. *BBC Online* said: "The set finishes predictably but majestically, with Queen's pomp-rock coup de grace: 'We Will Rock You', followed by 'We Are The Champions' and 'God Save The Queen'. If you need a reminder of just how invincible Queen were in concert, look no further."

AllMusic's Stephen Thomas Erlewine wrote: "Perhaps this isn't a definitive live statement – something that the band still doesn't have and still sorely needs – but it is a spirited, satisfying concert album that will please fans who still hunger for new Queen material years after Mercury's death."

A live tour was planned for 2005 and 2006. It was Queen's first tour since 1986. The band's final shows were at Wembley Stadium and lastly, Knebworth. Queen could not got further away from Freddie Mercury with such a raspy bluesy singer as Rodgers. The trio was joined by Queen's long-tome keyboard player Spike Edney, rhythm guitarist Jamie Moses and bassist Danny Miranda.

"We were appearing on a TV show together, The Music Hall of Fame, and the guys said to me 'if you will be our singer, we'll back you', and it went so well, that it went further,," Rodgrrs said to *Milton Keynes Citizen* in 2006. "I thought that we would get together and do a couple of shows, but when they said about a European tour it was a bit of a shock. I think that if I'd been asked without us having played together I would have hesitated..."

They made their first public performance at Nelson Mandela's 46664 AIDS concert in South Africa where Queen had controversially performed during the apartheid era in the 1980s.

"Me and Freddie are very different singers, and we work from different scales," Rodgers said to *Classic Rock's* Geoff Barton in 2005. "Freddie had more of a classic scale: do-re-mi-fa-so-la-ti-do, that sort of thing. Mine is more of a blues scale with a bit of Celtic thrown in. So there was that adjustment to make. I think, and I hope, that Freddie would approve."

There was a lot of material for the band to play around

with.

"It's still slightly fluid, to be honest. We've rehearsed more songs than we're actually going to be playing. But if you really want to know, I suppose it's about 65 per cent Queen and, and... erm, hang on a minute... 35 percent Paul," May said to Geoff Barton of *Classic Rock* about the forth coming road jaunt. "Something like that. But really we haven't solidified the set yet. It's close."

The tour kicked off at London 's Brixton Academy which was for Queen fan club members only. They played sold out arenas all around the UK.

The BBC's Janine Blinston said of the band's show at the Manchester Arena in May: "If anyone came to see Queen's greatest hits live, they would not have been disappointed, but a decent tribute band would have provided a more authentic Queen experience, with a Freddie-esque front man. This gig was an opportunity to do something different with some of the original Queen material. And it worked. A truly memorable experience and a more than adequate substitute for those of us too young to have seen the full band live in their prime. Freddie would be proud."

In Newcastle they performed Cream's 'Sunshine Of Your Love' in tribute to the Cream reunion concerts at London's Royal Albert Hall.

Stadium shows were played in Portugal, Germany and the Netherlands.

The band's gig at Lisbon's Estadio Do Restelo on July 2, 2005 was linked to Live 8, a follow up to Live Aid where Queen had stolen the show and made rock history with a truly monumental performance from the band, especially Freddie. The band dedicated 'Say It's Not True' and ''39' to Live 8. The former was written by Taylor about HIV/AIDS in Africa while the latter is an old May classic.

The band returned to England to perform an outdoor show at London's Hyde Park in front of over 60,000 fans in the summer of 2005. Free tickets were given away to the emergency services in the aftermath of the 7 July 2005 London bombings. Comedian Peter Kay and rock band Razorlight opened the show.

Paul Rodgers spoke to Geoff Barton of *Classic Rock* about the concert. "I was thinking today that I've lived about eight lifetimes. Here I am, I'm 55 years old, and I feel like I'm 17 again, starting a brand new career. It is quite incredible. We put the Hyde Park show in because the UK tour had sold out so quickly. A lot of people didn't get the opportunity to buy tickets; it took them – and us – by surprise. It'll be a great thrill; it'll be the first time I've played Hyde Park."

The set-lists were made up of the usual Queen classics from 'Bohemian Rhapsody' to 'Another One Bites The Dust', 'We Will Rock You', 'We Are The Champions' and 'A Kind Of Magic' et al. They also performed Free and Bad Company numbers such as 'All Right Now', 'Can't Get Enough' 'Wishing Well' and 'Bad Company'. Taylor sang 'These Are The Days Of Our Lives', 'I'm In Love With My Car', 'Radio Ga Ga' and 'Say It's Not True' while May sang ''39', 'Love Of My Life' and part of 'Hammer To Fall'.

They also surprised fans with some lesser known Queen songs such as 'I Was Born To Love You', 'Teo Torriatte', 'Too Much Love Will Kill You' and 'Dragon Attack'.

The band headed to the US for two LA shows at the end of the year. Guns N' Roses guitarist Slash joined them onstage for a version of 'Can't Get Enough' at the Hollywood Bowl.

Of the band's show at the Hollywood Bowl in October '05, *Variety*'s Steven Mirkin said: "While the show is billed as 'Queen+Paul Rodgers', about a third of the two-hour show subtracts Rodgers from the equation, as he gives way to solo showcases by May and Taylor. The latter takes a Gene Krupa-style drum solo that leads into 'I'm In Love With My Car' and comes out from behind the drum kit for a tender 'These Are the Days of Our Lives'. He's got such an attractively grainy voice you have to wonder why Queen doesn't consider going the Genesis route and turn him into their lead singer. May is attractively low-key on a folky 'Hammer to Fall' and a tousled ''39', but his extended guitar solos serve as a reminder that the excesses of '70s rock have not all aged equally well."

The collaboration saw the release of the live album and DVD *Return Of The Champions* in 2005; recorded in Sheffield on May 9, 2005.

Reviews were not great.

AllMusic's Stephen Thomas Erlewine wrote: "The end result is jarring, but not overly so: it's listenable, because the band is in good form, but apart from some nice work from May, *Return Of The Champions* never feels like Queen, it feels like a bar-band tribute band given a chance to play a big theater. Listening to the album, you get the sense that it probably was a fun night out, but there's no reason to listen to it at home."

Robert Christgau said: "Where Freddie Mercury was a true queen, Paul Rodgers is a big disgrace. And that's not even counting the Bad Company cover, the Free cover, or, facts is facts, the HIV song. D+"

The lengthy road jaunt was divided into three parts: Europe, Japan and the USA in 2006. The US tour lasted for 23 shows; the band's first shows since 1982 after which Queen ditched North America entirely to focus on Europe and South America.

Speaking about the collaborations future, Rodgers told Morley Seaver of *Anti Music*: "Well it's a kind of a go with the flow situation. We haven't a plan. We didn't really plan a world tour. It just kinda grew into that. Since then…the relationship is great. We've been in the studio and recorded some things, just to kind of suck it and see as they say, kinda situation and see what we put together, cause we've been around the world playing basically our hits, you know. And we did do one new song in North America, a song I wrote called 'Take Love' and so it remains to be seen what we can create, and it's exciting too because we don't really know. We go in there and say okay, what do you got? (laughs) We just kick something around and see where it takes us. We're just the three of us in the studio and we're kinda sharing the bass honours. Brian's doing some and I'm doing some, and it turns out actually Roger is a, I mean a great drummer. This we know. A great singer. This we know. He's a great songwriter. This we know. And he's also a fantastic guitar player."

With such a staggering back catalogue between both artists choosing song material for the live shows must have been a nightmare.

Of the setlists Rodgers said to *Glide Magazine*'s Leslie Michele Derrough: "When we first talked about doing something together, Brian May and Roger Taylor said to me, 'We would do half of your songs and half of our songs.' But at the time, I said, 'Now, you guys haven't been on the road for a long, long time and everybody is waiting for Queen. So we'll make it Queen heavy.' As a result of that, we only did five or six of my songs but they did them fantastically well. We did 'All Right Now', 'Feel Like Making Love', 'Shooting Star',

'Wishing Well' and they did a great version of my songs. But looking back, yeah, maybe we should have done more of mine. But it was a great experience and I loved it."

In the US Greg Schmitt wrote of the band's show in Worcester, MA for *Rockeyez*: "The night eventually crescendoed with Queen's crowning triumph, 'Bohemian Rhapsody'. As the image of the late, great Freddie Mercury appeared on screen, the band followed his lead, playing along to the interactive footage before dropping out on the operatic middle part, the way Queen has always done live. The band eventually returned for the big finale, with Paul and Freddie trading off lines as the majestic and touching tribute came to a close. Anyone cynically dismissing Queen + Paul Rodgers as a tribute act would be missing the point. Instead, it was a wonderful celebration of the regal catalog these artists represent. They will always be a spiritual treasure to millions and should never be hidden away because of the tragic loss of their leader."

Queen attended the VH1 Rock Honours awards in Las Vegas on May 25, 2006 where they were one of the recipients. The shows was opened by the Foo Fighters who performed 'Tie Your Mother Down' before Queen + Paul Rodgers joined them onstage for some other Queen songs,

It was a total shock to fans when Brian May confirmed via his popular website on August 15, 2006 that the band would be recording a new album.

The trio produced the album themselves with the help of Joshua J Macrae, Justin Shirley Smith and Kris Fredriksson. The album was recorded between Number 2007 and August 2008 at Roger Taylor's Priory studio. The recording sessions took place around Rodgers' solo shows. With the omission of John Deacon, Taylor and May took over bass duties.

"The song 'Voodoo', I had written that and we were just kicking ideas around when we played it," Rodgers said to Nick Deriso of *Something Else*. "It had such a great groove to it, but Brian always said to me: 'I can't really play blues.' I said: 'Yes, you can. Just play.' And he played a fantastic, very voodoo-like solo, right in the middle of it. I thought it was pretty good."

The band had debuted a new track called 'Take Love' on tour but it did not make it to the album. Rodgers, meanwhile, performed 'Warboys' and 'Voodoo' on his solo tour.

2006 saw the release of *Super Live In Japan*; a

Japanese only release.

In 2007 Queen revisited the past with the release of *Queen Rock Montreal*.

AllMusic's Stephen Thomas Erlewine wrote: "This double-disc contains the full set, including the previously unreleased 'Flash' and 'The Hero', and it benefits from the ebb and flow of a full concert, giving a broader, fuller sense of Queen at the peak of their power, which they were close to being at the time this was recorded. That is, they were close to the peak of their powers as world-conquering stadium rockers, touring the same set across the globe, perfecting it so it could play in any territory, as if it was rock & roll Esperanto."

The band performed at the 90th Birthday Party of Nelson Mandela at London's Hyde Park on June 27, 2008. The show was also staged to help elevate AIDS and HIV awareness. They performed 'One Vision', 'Tie Your Mother Down', 'The Show Must Go On', 'We Will Rock You', 'We Are the Champions' and 'All Right Now'.

The Cosmos Rocks was released on September 12, 2008 in Europe and October 28 in the USA. It reached Number 5 in the UK and 47 in the US.

The album's first single 'Say It's Not True' was released nine months before the album while the second single 'C-Lebrity' was released five months before the album. The band appeared on *Al Murray's Happy Hour* in April to promote it. Foo Fighters' drummer Taylor Hawkins appears on 'C-Lebrity' providing backing vocals.

Reviews were decidedly mixed.

Alexis Petridis of *The Guardian* wrote in his 2/5 review: "the lyrics were stupid, trite, a bit offensive and bound to have an undermining effect on whatever musical efforts they put behind it."

Lana Cooper of *Popmatters* wrote: "There won't ever be another Freddie Mercury, so why bother trying to replace him. Although his ghost pleasantly haunts the album in some ways (*The Cosmos Rocks* is actually dedicated to him), Paul Rodgers breathes new life into Queen, while still keeping the band's tremendous legacy intact as they soldier forth with new material into the 21st century."

Mojo gave it three stars: "Occasionally they stumble, as on the clunky 'Warboys'. But with Rodgers imperious, Queen's second coming is vindicated."

The band announced their second world tour, which opened on Kharkiv's Freedom Square in the Ukraine in front of a staggering 350,000 people. It was released on DVD in 2009.

Mike Ladano wrote: "There is also a center ramp that takes the members right into the crowd. I have always liked Paul's slant on Freddy's songs. He's not the same singer, not in the slightest, so the vocals lines change organically and it works. Unfortunately 'One Vision' is shortened so as to lead into 'Tie Your Mother Down' which is right up Paul's alley. Brian and Roger do their share of the backing vocals, and it sounds pretty Queen-like. (The live band is rounded out by longtime sideman Spike Edney (keyboards), Danny Miranda (bass) and Jamie Moses (backing guitar.))"

Paul Roy of *Blogcritics* said: "There were a few surprises this night including May's gorgeous performance of 'Last Horizon', which comes from his 1993 solo album, *Back To The Light*, as well as the *Innuendo* track, 'Bijou', where May played along to some old footage of Freddy Mercury singing it on the big screen. This made up for a pretty uninspired guitar solo that preceded them, where it sounded more like an exercise in how much delay effect May could use with without actually traveling back in time. ''39' sounded brilliant this night with May sitting at the front of the stage strumming an acoustic guitar and singing lead while Taylor sat to his right on the kick drum and tambourine. After a minute or so they bring out the rest of the support band to add some upright bass, accordion, and a second acoustic guitar to the mix."

The band also played shows in Russia. Further shows were staged around Europe before heading to the UK. They finished up in South America.

Of the band's show in Newcastle, England in November 2008, Dave Simpson of *The Guardian* said in his 2/5 review: "Paul Rodgers (bit of a pub rocker, competent, heterosexual) makes a decent fist of the blokey anthems like 'Radio Ga Ga' and' Tie Your Mother Down', while ghastly new material from *The Cosmos Rocks* album prompts a shuffle to the toilets. Mercury's subversive, sexual element is also lost, although Rodgers' multi-zipped trousers make lyrics like 'flying so low' sound like a reference to a wardrobe malfunction."

Throughout the Rock The Cosmos Tour the band performed to close to a million people playing 40 shows in total.

The collaboration came to a somewhat abrupt but

amicable end on May 12, 2009. Rodgers told *Billboard*: "At this point we're gonna sit back from this. My arrangement with (Queen's Brian May and Roger Taylor) was similar to my arrangement with Jimmy (Page) in The Firm in that it was never meant to be a permanent arrangement. I think we made a huge success of it, actually. We did two world tours and a couple of live recordings, and...made a studio album [...] which was pretty historical for (Queen's Brian May and Roger Taylor) because they hadn't really gone in the studio with anybody and recorded something like that for a very long time. So it was quite an achievement, I think."

"It's kind of an open book, really," he added, on the possibility of a reunion. "If they approach me to do something for charity, for instance, or something like that...I'd be very much into doing that, for sure."

It's very unlikely they will reunite.

"Being in a band is all-consuming and I like to have a life," Rodgers said to *Spinner* in 2012. "After leaving Queen I decided to stop doing those mega-four-month tours. I go out for a month and my dog recognizes me when I come home."

Harry Doherty said of the collaboration in 2010: "Live,

it worked amazingly well. The shows last year at the O2 were excellent, and he did make the role of lead singer his own, though no-one could match Freddie; and that Ukraine DVD is very, very good. I gave *The Cosmos Rocks* album a very good review in *Classic Rock*, but in retrospect, I think it flattered to deceive. It just doesn't have any longevity, not like the great Queen albums. It's a good idea that the project is now over."

Rodgers felt the same way about the live shows as he elaborated to *Milton Keynes Citizen* in 2006: "It was in Vancouver and it was so great. It was like all of the other shows on the tour had been a practice for this one. Quite often at the end of a tour you are quite jaded, but everyone was on fire. If you measure us on a scale of one to ten, we generally hit eight and a half, average. But this night? We were on eleven!"

It was a worthwhile collaboration for Rodgers which gave him more than expected.

Rodgers later said to Nick Deriso of *Something Else*: "I think Elton John described it [Queen] as having a fantastic car in the garage, but with one part missing — so you can't take it out, you know? They had all of the machinery: They had all of those songs, wonderful musicians, a great light show. It's all ready to go, but they were missing that one piece, which was the frontman singing. There wasn't anyone who was really willing to pick up that baton, and run with it. I did, and we did that together — and it lasted a lot longer than I had planned. Originally, we were just going to do a tour of Europe just for fun, because it was so enjoyable to play together. And that turned into four years, during which we toured the world twice, and I went to all kinds of places I had never been before. We recorded a few live DVDs and finished off with a studio album of original material, at which time I felt it was time for me to get back, full on, to be own thing — my own music."

After the collaboration came to a stop Queen announced the release of a greatest hits collection called *Absolute Queen* which was issued in November 2009. The album features 20 tracks and prior to its release the band ran a competition online for fans to guess the track-listing.

In a letter to the band's fanclub Brian May wrote on October 30, 2009: "The greatest debate, though, is always about when we will next play together as Queen. At the moment, in spite of the many rumours that are out there, we do not have plans to tour in 2010. The good news, though, is that Roger and I have a much closer mutual understanding these days—privately and professionally ... and all ideas are carefully considered. Music is never far away from us. As I write, there is an important one-off performance on offer, in the USA, and it remains to be decided whether we will take up this particular challenge. Every day, doors seem to open, and every day, we interact, perhaps more than ever before, with the world outside. It is a time of exciting transition in Rock music and in 'The Business'. It's good that the pulse still beats."

They appeared onstage on November 15, 2009 on *The X-Factor* with the finalists.

The band also released another compilation; this time called *Absolute Greatest*. The collection received mostly positive reviews; though there is only so many times a band can release collections featuring mostly the same tracks. Had the band exhausted their back catalogue? Post Freddie, the band had released many more compilations around the world. Too many to get bogged down with here.

May and Taylor announced on May 7, 2010 that they were leaving EMI, their record label of four decades. It was confirmed by their long-time manager Jim Beach that the band were signing a new deal with Universal Music; more specifically an sub-company Island Records. It marked the first time since the 1980s that the band's music had the same record label worldwide. In the USA they had been distributed by Hollywood Records (Universal) and before that Capitol Records in the eighties which was owned by EMI.

"The regular back catalog is already out there. Hollywood Records have done a fantastic job in the States with it," May told *Goldmine*'s Dave Thompson. "I'm amazed, really, all the more so since Capitol failed so hugely with it when we were signed with them a while ago. I think the difference was, Hollywood are rather intelligent and don't make a huge hoohah and get on with the job and do it pretty well. So that's taken care of."

The band began a campaign to release all their albums via Universal. The first wave was issued in March; the second wave in June and the final wave in September. They were released as remastered deluxe editions.

Jane's Addiction singer Perry Farrell said in May 2011 that Queen were attempting to recruit their live bassist Chris Chaney.

So all in all the Queen + Paul Rodgers collaboration took place between 2004 and 2009 and spawned two major world tours and a lukewarmly received album called *The Cosmos Rocks* as well as a live album called *Return Of The Champions* and a CD and DVD named *Live In Ukraine*.

What would May and Taylor do next?

PHOTO BY NOEL BUCKLEY

PHOTO BY NOEL BUCKLEY

PHOTO BY NOEL BUCKLEY

PHOTO BY NOEL BUCKLEY

NEIL DANIELS

PHOTO BY NOEL BUCKLEY

PHOTO BY NOEL BUCKLEY

NEIL DANIELS

PHOTO BY NOEL BUCKLEY

QUEEN + ADAM LAMBERT

Queen's first meeting with Adam Lambert actually happened back in May 2009 when on the twentieth *American Idol* finalists Adam Lambert and Kris Allen and Brian May and Roger Taylor of Queen performed 'We Are The Champions' during the finale.

"Oh my god, what an honour," he said to *Entertainment Weekly*'s Adam B. Vary in 2009. "Queen is like one of my all time favourite rock bands, and then to be up on stage with KISS with the pyro and the costumes – I mean, it was a dream come true. It was awesome."

Unfortunately Lambert did not win the competition, losing to Kris Allen and coming second in the overall votes.

"The first thing I did in the morning was crack a Red Bull," he said to *Rolling Stone*'s Vanessa Grigoriadis in 2009 about the morning after the finale. "For a little while, I felt I was at a rave. Then I went from 'Oh, my God, who has glow sticks?' to 'Stick a pacifier in me, I'm done.'"

During Lambert's run on *American Idol* he sang a variety of songs either solo or in a group efforts, those numbers included 'Rock With You' by Michael Jackson, Queen's 'Bohemian Rhapsody', 'What's Up' by 4 Non Blondes, 'Some Kind Of Wonderful' by Soul Brothers Six, Cher's 'Believe', Rolling Stones' ('I Can't Get No) Satisfaction', Michael Jackson's 'Black Or White', Anita Carter /Johnny Cash's 'Ring Of Fire', 'Tracks Of My Years' by The Miracles, 'Play That Funky Music' by Wild Cherry, 'Mad World' (originally by Tears For Fears), 'Born To Be Wild' by Steppenwolf, 'If I Can't Have You' by Yvonne Elliman, 'Feeling Good' by Cy Grant, 'Whole Lotta Love' by Led Zeppelin and Foghat's 'Slow Ride', 'One' by U2 and Aerosmith's 'Cryin'', 'A Change Is Gonna Come' by Sam Cooke' and the original AI single 'No Boundaries' as well as Queen's 'We Are The Champions' with Queen and KISS's 'Beth', 'Detroit Rock City' and 'Rock And Roll All Nite' with KISS.

His favourite rock singers include Freddie Mercury, David Bowie and Robert Plant. Growing up he was a huge fan of the British glam rock scene of the 1970s especially the Ziggy Stardust era of Bowie's career. He would spend hours listening to Queen and mimic the vocals of Freddie Mercury, though he did not properly devour the band's music until his early twenties. The flamboyance of Mercury and Bowie also had a profound impact on Lambert.

Like many of his American peers, Lambert first discovered Queen after watching the 'Bohemian Rhapsody' scene in the 1992 Mike Myers and Dana Carvey comedy *Wayne's World*. He asked his dad about the song and his dad told him that they wrote 'We Will Rock You' and 'We Are The Champions'.

Queen's career in the US had taken a nose-dive after 'I Want To Break Free', a famous music video where members of the band dress as women mimicking the British TV soap *Coronation Street.* Middle America thought that Mercury might actually be gay. The band didn't want to work so hard to get their audiences back and so they concentrated on other parts of the world where they were filling stadiums and selling millions of albums. They hoped a hit record would resurrect their career in America. It didn't happen. However, *Wayne's World* and the publicity surrounding Mercury's death did boost their appeal in the US which is when Lambert and other music fans his age learned about them.

"When I was older I got more into the history of rock,"

he said to *Rolling Stone*'s Andy Greene in 2014. "I fell in love with the 1970s and I discovered more about Queen. The genius about the band is that they're so versatile. There are songs in their catalog that are like beautiful lullabies, and then on the same album they can flip to a hardcore, more aggressive sound."

Many of his musical heroes came out of the 1970s, mostly from the glam scene in England or in Detroit and New York.

"What's funny is that in the '70s a lot of the glam artists – like Bowie, T. Rex, Iggy Pop, Alice Cooper, KISS – they were gender bending with their image, but most of them were pretty hetero." *Out*'s Shana Naomi Krochmal in 2009. "Even though they looked really flamboyant. Bowie was the one guy that kind of made you wonder. But he was straight, right?"

His obvious love of classic rock and pop is what would help him carve out a career in the music industry, and ultimately what would make his name on his major breakthrough, which was just a round the corner.

Lambert joined the remaining members of Queen, Brian May and Roger Taylor, in November 2011 for a performance of 'The Show Must Go On', 'We Will Rock You' and 'We Are The Champions' at the 2011 MTV Europe Music Awards in Belfast. Queen were handed the 'Global Icon Award'. Roger Taylor admitted in December that Queen were in talks with Lambert over a possible collaboration.

"There was stuff I really wanted to do on my own first," he admitted to *Rolling Stone*'s Andy Greene in 2014. "But there was definitely interest from me and the band. When we finally got together at the MTV Video Music Awards about a year or two after *Idol* it felt like the right time to start talking, since I'd established my solo career."

Queen appeared on the eleventh series of *American Idol* on April 25 and 26 2011 where they performed a medley of their hits with the six finalists, They played 'Somebody To Love' the following day with the official tribute band, Queen Extravaganza.

2011 saw the release of three compilations of classic Queen Materia under the *Deep Cuts* moniker. They featured some of the band's lesser-known songs.

After much press hype it was announced in February 2012 that Lambert would unite with Queen to headline the UK's Sonisphere Festival held at Knebworth in July, however, it the entire festival was axed. Roger Taylor quickly announced that the band would perform with Lambert in Moscow with the addition of two shows in London and one in Kiev at Independence Square which would also feature Elton John as headliner in aid of the Elena Pinchuk ANTIAIDS Foundation. A fifth gig was added in Wroclaw while a third London show was added after the first two sold out.

"I still can't believe we're doing this," Lambert said to *Digital Spy*'s Robert Copsey. "It'll sink in eventually! All we've done is send a couple of emails back and forth, but we'll get down to serious rehearsals soon. They're such sweet guys – almost paternal – and they're doing this for the right reasons. They love what they do and they want to keep giving to the fans."

The Queen + Adam Lambert collaboration brought the singer to the forefront of the rock music press. Mercury would probably approve of Lambert, at least as far as Lambert and many Queen fans think, though there will also be sceptics.

"I'm an artist, you know," he expressed to the *Village Voice*'s Maura Johnston in 2012. "My goal is to do the songs justice and not stray too far. I don't want to sacrilege; I want to keep the intent. I mean, I have Brian and Roger on stage, in rehearsal, telling me green light or red light. So I'm going to look to them in hopes of being kinda like, 'Hey, is this cool?' And I'm their guest."

The mini-tour commenced in Kiev with their first full gig as Q+AL on June 30 the night before the Euro 2012 Football Championship. The Moscow gig took place on July 3 at Olympic Stadium while the Poland event on July 7 took place at Municpal Stadium. The collaboration took some heavy criticism in the UK where Lambert was not so well known and where Queen are hailed as one of the greatest rock bands in the world. Why would they hire a former *American Idol* contestant to front the band?

Nevertheless three sold out Hammersmith Apollo gigs took place on July 11, 12, and 14.

"It's probably a dream come true for Adam, but I wonder if he has the groundwork to see him through a big tour with those guys," Paul Rodgers said to *Spinner* in 2012.

The London shows featured classic Queen songs in a truly awesome setlist: 'Flash' (intro), 'Seven Seas Of Rhye', 'Keep Yourself Alive', 'We Will Rock You' (fast version), 'Fat

Bottomed Girls', 'Don't Stop Me Now', 'Under Pressure', 'I Want It All', 'Who Wants To Live Forever', 'A Kind Of Magic', 'These Are The Days Of Our Lives', 'Somebody To Love', 'Love Of My Life', ''39', 'Dragon Attack', 'I Want To Break Free', 'Another One Bites The Dust', 'Radio Ga Ga', 'Crazy Little Thing Called Love', 'The Show Must Go On' and 'Bohemian Rhapsody' with an encore of 'Tie Your Mother Down', 'We Will Rock You' and 'We Are The Champions' with the usual recorded climax to a Queen show, 'God Save The Queen'.

The reviews were much better than expected, as evidenced here:

The Guardian's Caroline Sullivan reviewed one of the London gigs: "It's no insult to Lambert, a theatrical pop star in his own right, to say he lacks Mercury's magisterial authority. The late singer still inhabits every one of Queen's songs, and the best Lambert could do was sing them with verve. While vocally equal to the crescendos and curlicues, he was unable to compete with Mercury's memory – something vividly proved during 'Love Of My Life', when 1980s footage of Mercury unexpectedly flashed on screen. The crowd's gasp spoke volumes."

The Daily Telegraph's Neil McCormick wrote: "Hand-picked by guitarist Brian May, Lambert can certainly handle the vocal range of Queen's songs although he sings in a softer, more soulful, modern pop style, without Mercury's rock grit or operatic bombast."

He continued: "But it is to his credit that he is a talent in his own right and not just an impersonator. If his performance seems to improve as the show goes on, it's hard to be sure if that is a sign of Lambert finding his mojo, or the audience tuning in to his particular brand of flamboyant showmanship."

Indulge-Sound's Emma Webb enthused: "It was clear to see that having Adam fronting Queen for these shows was a spectacularly brilliant choice of vocalist; with his own little twist on songs including a sped up version of 'We Will Rock You' and providing us with a British accent before belting out 'Fat Bottomed Girls', he did not want to mimic Freddie (as let's face it, no one can) but he merely wanted to do him, the fans and the band proud and he went down a glamorous treat."

Lambert was praised by his friends and collaborators too.

"Pharrell [Williams] and I started talking and he said I was our generations Freddie Mercury," Lambert told celebrity gossip writer Dean Piper. "That was ridiculous. You're never going to replace Freddie in any way. But I'm thrilled to have the chance to do stuff with them. I can't wait to work with them again."

Adam Lambert is far more suited to the look and sound of Queen than former Free and Bad Company singer Paul Rodgers.

"Paul has one of the greatest rock voices but it's more blues- and soul-orientated I would have thought," Taylor told the *Toronto Sun*. "I would say, with all due respect to Paul, that Adam is more suited to a lot of our material and whereas we had great tours with Paul, I think Adam is more naturally at home with us."

"Yeah, I think the styles match more closely in a sense," May echoed to the *Toronto Sun*. "But we had a great time with Paul, no doubt about it, and it kind of stretched it to a new place and, I think, a thoroughly good experience. But Adam is really… Like us, he has many, many colours, so we can explore some of those strange excursions that Queen likes to."

It is clear that not only do May and Taylor appreciate and admire Lambert as a singer and artist but they also like him as a person.

Reflecting on the collaboration, Brian May spoke to *Ultimate Classic Rock*'s Annie Zaleski in 2013: "I would love it to happen. Since we did the iHeartRadio Festival, there's been a lot of talk and yes, we're looking at it to see what we could do. I don't think we want to press the button to do nine months on the road like we used to do, because we did that for so many years, but I think a few choice dates could be great. We're looking at it, and I certainly hope that we'd be able to come up with a scheme that works. Yeah, we love Adam, we really do. Like you say, he's the whole deal – he's an extraordinary singer with an extraordinary instrument. He's an entertainer, he's original and he's a nice guy. That's very important these days. If you're going to work with someone, you've got to enjoy them as a person and we certainly do."

2012 saw the release of some vintage material with *Hungarian Rhapsody: Queen Live In Budapest*.

After the Queen dates he continued his solo career which continued to thrive. Lambert collaborated again with

Queen on September 20 2013 on the closing night of the iHeartRadio Music Festival at Las Vegas' MGM Grand Arena. The festival was broadcast live on Clear Channel to 150 US markets.

Speaking to *Kings Of A&R* in 2011, guitarist and friend Monte Pittman enthused: "He recently played with Queen and I thought it was brilliant. It's a phenomenal experience seeing a friend achieve so much so quickly. He's really defined in what he wants and can be a perfectionist about it. You can hear for yourself when you hear him sing. I think he's out of everyone's league on that show."

The critics praised Q+AL's performance in Sin City.

Steve Baltin of *Grammy.com* enthused: "So much of the reason why this incarnation of Queen is exciting is Lambert, whose confidence and theatricality fit like a glove. While his admiration of Mercury is clear to see, he is wisely not trying to replace an irreplaceable legend. Of course, May and drummer Roger Taylor remain two of rock's finest at their respective instruments and they propel this version of Queen to lofty standards. That pedigree came through especially on the rock grandeur of 'Fat Bottomed Girls', but also on the musically bipolar 'Under Pressure', Queen's classic duet with David Bowie, which excelled with Taylor handling a majority of the vocals."

Hollywood Reporter's Shirley Halperin wrote: "Decked all in black and donning a pair of stylish, silvery platform shoes (presumably Louboutins, judging from their cherry red soles), Lambert sported a moustache that would have made the late Freddie Mercury proud. With the perfect mix of rock attitude mixed with style, theatricality, sex appeal and impressive vocal gymnastics, he took the band's music to new heights in front of a worldwide audience."

Billboard's Jason Lipshutz wrote: "With each new show, Lambert's involvement with the five-decade-old band makes more sense: Freddie Mercury's king-sized songwriting makes for a perfect vessel for Lambert's operatic wail, and iHeartRadio fest attendees who wanted to stick around for 'Another One Bites The Dust' got to witness the magnetic power of Lambert's pristine high notes. The former *American Idol* runner-up oozed charisma as he strutted around the stage, winking at his reputation of a fill-in while also reminding people they should still pay attention to his solo career whenever this stint with Queen, er, bites the dust."

They played an eight song setlist: 'We Will Rock You', 'Another One Bites The Dust', 'Crazy Little Thing Called Love', 'Love Kills', 'Fat Bottomed Girls', 'Under Pressure', 'We Are The Champions' and 'Don't Stop Me Now'.

It was announced on March 6 that a full scale North American Queen + Adam Lambert tour was taking place with 19 initial dates beginning in Chicago on June 19. It was announced on *Good Morning America* and at a press conference at Madison Square Garden. Lambert confirmed on March 15 that the Madison Square Garden gig had sold out in a day and that five extra shows had been added due to overwhelming demand.

Everything went well at the production rehearsals in London where they arranged the setlist and rehearsed for the tour. They geared the set towards the die-hard Queen fans and the more casual fans, so all the big hits are in the setlist as well as some lesser known tunes such as 'In The Lap Of The Gods' and 'Stone Cold Crazy'. One song they decided to adopt for the US setlist was 'Love Kills', a 1984 Freddie Mercury track that was recorded with Giorgio Moroder for the remastered and restored version of Fritz Lang's 1927 silent sci-fi masterpiece,

Metropolis. They took out the disco element and made it more of a traditional Queen song, which is included on the recent compilation *Queen Forever*. It was an exciting albeit nerve-wrecking period for Lambert. To go from auditioning for *American Idol* back in 2009 with 'Bohemian Rhapsody' to actually fronting Queen is an unbelievable journey.

The one thing Lambert wanted to stress was that he is in by no means replacing Mercury. He knew enough and is talented enough to both honour Mercury yet add his own style to the songs.

"I remember seeing some footage of him and thinking, 'Wow, this guy is on fire! What an amazing performer!'" he said to the *Advocate*'s Daniel Reynolds in 2014.

Entertainment Weekly's Erika Berlin raved over the band's performance at the sold out Madison Square Garden gig: "So while his skinny leather pants, leopard-print tuxes, and use of studs and fringe in a single outfit would likely all be Freddie-approved, Adam Lambert was very much his glam-punk self, and Mercury still kept a couple of coveted solos for himself."

Also reviewing said Madison Square Garden gig, *New York Daily News*' Kevin Coughlin: "Last, but certainly not the least, former *American Idol* finalist Adam Lambert channels the spirit of Queen's late frontman Freddie Mercury in almost every detail. Strutting the curvaceous stage like a black leather-clad peacock with a slight pompadour, Lambert launched into the set opener, 'Now I'm Here' with ferocity and vigour. At times, Lambert's presence appeared to rejuvenate and energize May's and Taylor's performance throughout the 2 hour 15-minute, 23-song set."

They were also set to play at The Forum in Los Angeles where the band had last performed in 1982.

"It's a great place to be; I feel so fortunate to be going out there. I never thought it would happen again," May explained to Eddie Trunk on *That Metal Show*. "When Freddie went, I thought: 'That's it. We did that. It was a great life. Now, it's time to have a different life.' And for years, we didn't try to be Queen in any way. I would look at the Forum in LA, and I would look at Madison Square Garden, and I would think: 'Those were the days.' To come back now, all of these years later, and to fill those places and to hear that noise. That's vindication for the fact that we should be playing, we should be out there. I feel overcome with it, really."

Having retired from the music scene Queen bassist John Deacon declined to take part, having not been directly involved with the band since 1997. Joining May, Taylor and Lambert was long-time keyboardist Spike Edney, bassist Neil Fairclough and percussionist Rufus Tiger Taylor (Roger Taylor's son).

"After we lost Freddie, there was a long period for Roger and I where we didn't want to talk about it," May admitted to *Planet Rock*'s Nicky Horne. "That was a part of our lives that we had done, and now we were individuals. But it comes back, because people actually do want to hear the music. We're still able to play, and we can bring Freddie back and we can bring John back – even though neither of them are with us on stage, technically. Spiritually, they are."

They took the tour around the world when they headlined Korea's Super Sonic 2014 festival in Seoul in August (Queen had never played Korea) and Japan's Summer Sonic 2014 festival in Osaka and Tokyo on August 16 and 17 where they had last performed eight years previously with Paul Rodgers.

After thirty years, Queen were set to return to Australia

for the first time since 1985 after a tour was announced in May. The band announced an initial four dates with a further two shows added due to demand. It kicked off in Perth on August 22 and shows were staged in Sydney, Melbourne and Brisbane on September 1. Shows were also staged in New Zealand at Auckland's Vector Arena from September 3 to 4.

Daily Review's Ben Neutze reviewed one of the Sydney shows at the Allphones Arena: "When pop icon of the moment Lady Gaga (who took her name from the band's 1984 hit 'Radio Ga Ga') appeared onstage as a surprise guest to duet with Lambert on 'Another One Bites The Dust', we caught a glimpse of a similar kind of raw, unpredictable power, as she strutted and fidgeted around the stage and down the catwalk in an obnoxiously large black wig and skin-tight velvet bodysuit."

Noise 101's Paul Cashmere reviewed the band's visit to Melbourne on August 30 and wrote: "Adam Lambert does not try to replace Freddie Mercury, or invent the songs. He plays a humble alternative delivering these classics as they were originally intended."

The 35 date tour was a huge critical and commercial success. The North American and Oceania tour, according to

Pollstar, grossed $37 million and was ranked 35th in the Top 100 worldwide tours of 2014.

Roger Taylor raved about Lambert to *Ultimate Classic Rock*'s Matt Wardlaw: "I have to say, it was just great. You know, we got on so well with Adam. He fitted in so well with us and he brought so much to the show. [He's a] great frontman and he looked great and he sings beautifully, and his style is very suited to our music. You know, it's pretty theatrical music, some of our stuff. He's the greatest. So, we really had a ball and I think it came over in the shows. They were very well attended and the reception that we got in every city was great. So, it was a really great experience and I'm thrilled."

There's certainly a difference between singing Queen songs, many of which are universally well-known and without much effort encourage the audience to sing along and dance while his own solo work requires more work when involving the audience.

"It's a huge challenge as well, because there's been a lot of expectation and doubt," he said to the *Advocate*'s Daniel Reynolds in 2014. "You have a mix of people in the audience that are diehard Queen fans, and I have my fans that are coming to the show kind of through me. It's interesting bringing them all together and seeing how it all plays out."

The 2014 setlist looked like this 'Procession' (recorded intro), 'Now I'm Here', 'Stone Cold Crazy', 'Another One Bites The Dust', 'Fat Bottomed Girls', 'In The Lap Of The Gods...Revisited', 'Seven Seas Of Rhye', 'Killer Queen', 'Somebody To Love', 'I Want It All', 'Love Of My Life', ''39', 'These Are The Days Of Our Lives', (bass solo / drum battle) 'Under Pressure', 'Love Kills', 'Who Wants To Live Forever', (guitar solo) 'Last Horizon', 'Tie Your Mother Down', 'Radio Ga Ga' 'Crazy Little Thing Called Love', 'The Show Must Go On' and 'Bohemian Rhapsody' with an encore of 'We Will Rock You' and 'We Are The Champions' and the closing tape of 'God Save The Queen'.

Some shows featured ;'Don't Stop Me Now' in place of 'Radio Ga Ga' and 'Dragon Attack' instead of 'Love Kills'. They also played 'I Was Born To Love You' in Japan and even the Brian May penned 'Tea Torriatte'.

May told Japan's Universal Music: "They're difficult songs to sing, Queen songs. There's too much range. So many people can't sing them in the original key – even if they are good singers, Adam comes along, [and] he can do it easy. He can do it in his sleep! He can sing higher than even Freddie could in a live situation. So I think Freddie would look at this guy and think, 'Hmm… Yeah. Okay.' There would be a kind of, 'Hmm ... You bastard. You can do this.'"

After the tour came to an end he resumed work on his next solo opus.

"I think there will be, yeah. I'm working with an amazing executive producer," he said to US showbiz TV host Ryan Seacrest in September. "Again, I can't say too much, but it's gonna be really good."

Queen released the compilation *Queen Forever* in November 2014 which feature unreleased material and including the Mercury and Michael Jackson duet 'There Must Be More To Life Than This'. The album also features three new tracks which featured Mercury's vocals.

Daily Mail's David Bennun wrote: "As per its title, Queen Forever is a statement of intent. A classic act is no longer merely the sum of its parts and its works. It is an industry in itself, and self-perpetuating. Here Queen proclaim their right to live for ever – not just in popular memory, but at the tills and in the charts."

The Guardian's Dave Simpson wrote: "A consummate Freddie Mercury is at his most confident in opener 'Let Me in Your Heart Again', a huge piano- and guitar-driven power ballad from the sessions that produced 'Radio Ga Ga'. It sounds like the great Queen single that never was. Another gem is the band's version of 'Love Kills' – far more stripped down, raw and impassioned than the dancier, Giorgio Moroder-product solo hit for Mercury."

Helen Brown from *The Daily Telegraph* wrote: "More effective is Brian May's bombastic **'Let Me in Your Heart Again'**, on which the guitarist's fingers skid up the fretboard in a perfect echo of Mercury's 1984 vocal soaring up the octave. 'Love Kills', Mercury's rushed electronic collaboration with Giorgio Moroder, gets its power ballad sails filled by the band (minus bassist John Deacon)."

2014 also saw the release of *Live At The Rainbow '74*, an acclaimed classic Queen concert.

Joe Sweeny of *Popmatters* said: "But on the whole, you really can't go wrong here – skip the first set and you miss a scorching medley of 'Jailhouse Rock', 'Stupid Cupid', and 'Be-

Bop-A-Lula', for instance. *Live At The Rainbow '74* doesn't just succeed as an album full of raucous, fantastical, peerlessly executed rock and roll. It also thrills by pinpointing a place and time when a great band made the leap from the streets of London into the lap of the gods."

Jason Ritchie of *Get Ready To Rock* wrote: "Good sound quality too and of course the fun rock 'n' roll covers appear at the end of the set, 'Big Spender' (still performed by the band in their final shows in 1986) and 'Jailhouse Rock'. Queen fans will definitely want the March concert as it was pre-*Sheer Heart Attack* and includes the only known surviving live recording of 'The Fairy Feller's Master Stroke'. Fans are spoilt for choice really on formats although you do need both discs as a minimum just as a lasting memento of how the band started out.

On September 19 an initial 21 date UK and Europe tour for was announced that was set to cover ten countries beginning in January 2015. A second O2 show in London was added as other dates in the UK such as Liverpool due to overwhelming demand for tickets. The tour ventured to an eleventh country after it was announced they were set to play Krakow Arena in Poland bringing the tour to 26 dates. The 10th annual *Classic*

Rock Roll Of Honours Awards named Queen + Adam Lambert the 'Band Of The Year' on November 4.

The band made an appearance performing 'I Want It All' and 'Who Wants To Live Forever' on Helene Fischer's annual Christmas show on December 24 on Berlin before a performance of 'Somebody To Love' with contestants on the UK's *The X Factor*.

The *Daily Mirror*'s Sophia Rahman wrote about the band's appearance on the popular talent show: "Ageing rockers Queen and their quiffed singer Adam Lambert joined the contestants to open tonight's nail-biting show with a rousing performance of their classic 'Somebody To Love'. Judges Mel B, Cheryl, Simon and Louis gave a standing ovation to the foursome and Adam had some advice for the wannabe popstars. The be-quiffed singer told Dermot the hopefuls should 'be present in every moment and think ahead'."

It was announced that they were to play an exclusive New Year's Eve gig at London's Central Hall Westminster next to Big Ben to bring in the New Year. It was broadcast on BBC one and staged by BBC Music. The event was dubbed 'Queen + Adam Lambert Rock Big Ben Live' and was broadcast live from

23:15 to 00:30 with a pause between 23:59 to 00:10 to celebrate the New Year with a fireworks display above the River Thames.

The first part of the gig was seen by an average of 5.83 million people while the second part was seen by an estimated 10 million viewers. It was streamed live on BBC music and presented by presented by BBC Radio 1 DJ's Greg James and Gemma Cairney.

The setlist featured 'Don't Stop Me Now', 'I Want To Break Free', 'Somebody To Love', 'Another One Bites The Dust', 'Under Pressure', 'Fat Bottomed Girls', 'Radio Ga Ga', 'I Want It All', 'Crazy Little Thing Called Love' and 'The Show Must Go On' with an encore of 'Bohemian Rhapsody' and 'Killer Queen' (medley) and 'We Will Rock You' and 'We Are The Champions'. A recording of Freddie Mercury from Rock Montreal was shown during 'Bohemian Rhapsody' and the start of 'We Will Rock You' featured bagpipes.

The concert brought Lambert to the forefront of the UK public after it was announced he came up tops in the Goggle Trends searching list.

"It's not, in any sense, a copy," May told *Planet Rock*'s Nicky Horne of the Queen + Adam Lambert shows. "And it's a joy for me to explore this material with Adam. The final piece of the jigsaw puzzle is that he's a nice guy. If he was a shit, it wouldn't have been fun – and it wouldn't have happened. [Laughs.] He's a good guy, he's fun, he entertaining and he's open to ideas. And he bring lots of ideas in, so when we were putting this setlist together he didn't just go, 'OK, I'll do what you want.' He said, 'How about we try this? 'Let's do this.' So, we had a real proper birth process. It's great. I just feel very grateful, Nicky."

Queen + Adam Lambert appeared on the cover *Classic Rock* magazine in January.

The Queen tour in the UK and Europe, meanwhile, was going down a storm receiving rave reviews from fans and critics.

May praised Lambert's showmanship in an interview with Japan's Universal Music: "He doesn't have to try. He is a natural, in the same way that Freddie was…We didn't look for this guy, [but] suddenly he's there, and he can sing all of those lines... He doesn't imitate; he just does his own thing."

The 2015 setlist ran as follows: 'One Vision', 'Stone Cold Crazy', 'Another One Bites The Dust', 'Fat Bottomed Girls', 'In The Lap Of The Gods…Revisited', 'Seven Seas Of

Rhye', 'Killer Queen', 'I Want To Break Free', 'Don't Stop Me Now', 'Somebody To Love', 'Love Of My Life', ''39', 'These Are The Days Of Our Lives' (bass solo / drum battle) 'Under Pressure', 'Save Me', 'Who Wants To Live Forever', (guitar solo) 'Last Horizon', 'Tie Your Mother Down', 'I Want It All', 'Radio Ga Ga', 'Crazy Little Thing Called Love' and 'Bohemian Rhapsody' with an encore of 'We Will Rock You' and 'We Are The Champions' followed by a recording of 'God Save The Queen to close the show.

Some shows had 'A Kind Of Magic' in replace of 'These Are The Days Of Our Lives' and an addition of 'the Show Must Go On'.

Catherine Gee of *The Daily Telegraph* gave the band's performance at London's O2 Arena on January 17 4/5 and enthused: "At the time, Adam Lambert was just three years old. But it's his youth and rapturous energy that has given Queen the glittering boost that they've been so desperately lacking since Mercury's death. Without attempting to impersonate Mercury – if anything, he looks more like George Michael – Lambert has brought dazzling showmanship and style back to the band. He's also everything that Queen's last long-term singer, the blokey, bluesy, ex-Bad Company frontman Paul Rodgers, is not."

The Guardian's Dave Simpson said of the tour's opening night in Newcastle: "When Lambert claps hands, the audience clap with him, unprompted. His unusually wide vocal range allows him to hit high notes (notably Mercury's famous one in 'Somebody To Love') which would normally require the assistance of even tighter trousers."

He continued: "However, the Indianan is no mere talent show get-lucky. Like Mercury, Lambert paid his dues with opera training, theatre, singing in clubs and performing dance and rock, which has given him the dexterity to tackle a catalogue stretching from thumping grooves ('Radio Ga Ga', 'Another One Bites The Dust') to blistering hard rock ('Seven Seas of Rhye', 'Tie Your Mother Down')."

In Manchester, Katie Fitzpatrick of the *Manchester Evening News* raved: "He isn't meant to be a Freddie clone. But here is a charismatic singer who performs and celebrates Queen's timeless back catalogue, including 'Another One Bites The Dust', 'Tie Your Mother Down' and 'Fat Bottomed Girls', exactly the way they should be with added new electricity."

In Leeds, the *Daily Express*' Paul Jeeves wrote: "Every

song is a nailed-on humdinger of a classic and yet it is this, and the lack of odd curveball or rarity, that perhaps creates the West End vibe of the concert. In many ways this is the ultimate homage to Queen and with that in mind, Lambert is as good as it is going to get for fans who yearn for the impossible. And when the song is right boy can this fella sing. He holds all the notes in all the right places and his range is more than impressive. 'I Want It All', 'Radio GaGa', 'Crazy Little Thing Called Love' all fit Lambert's vocals like a glove and as the crowd embraces him his charisma shines through."

However, the band were forced to cancel the planned Brussels show after Lambert was diagnosed with severe bronchitis and was ordered 24 hour vocal and bed rest by a doctor. Because of the unavailability of the venue they were unable to reschedule and so the show had to be axed entirely. He tweeted: "Thanks for the well wishes guys! Send me some healing energy, I'll drink a ton of water and sleep! Sound like a plan?" and "Brussels: sad we had to cancel tonight. The last thing I'd want is to let u down but I'm under doctors' orders to stay in bed and get well. Thank you for your understanding and patience. ;)"

Q+AL brought an end to their sold-out European tour at Sheffield Motorpoint Arena on Feb 27. However it did not prove to be the end of the collaboration. A press release was published on February 27, part of which read: "Following 67 sold-out concerts performed together around the world, Queen + Adam Lambert head to South America to top the opening night at Rock in Rio Brazil '30 Years Celebration' edition on Friday September 18."

And continued: "Rio de Janeiro, February, 26th, 2015 – Says Rock in Rio President and Founder Roberto Medina: '30 years ago, Queen performed in front of 250,000 people who fell in love with the band, and it became one of the most iconic moments of Rock in Rio. I am positive that the moments from 30 years ago will be rejuvenated and rejoiced with Queen + Adam Lambert, making it again a moment no one will ever forget.'"

What an incredible opportunity for both Adam Lambert and Queen.

Q+AL have not announced plans for any more shows the release of their first live album and DVD but they have suggested the possibility of some new studio material.

"It really is a dream job, and it's really cool," he enthused to Matthew Breen of the *Advocate* in 2011. "I do stop and keep it all in perspective. This is pop music, and it's not fucking brain surgery. I mean, some of it's serious…but some of it's just really fun dance music. And I'm wearing eight pounds of makeup because I fucking want to. Why not?"

There's a fine balancing act between artistic creativity and freedom and making money and selling records. Artists have to make a living too. It took time for Lambert to figure out the business but he remains surrounded by good people who keep him grounded and whose advice he respects.

2015 also saw the release of yet more vintage concert music with *A Night At The Odeon – Hammersmith 1975*.

Matt Collar of *AllMusic* wrote: "As live Queen albums go, *A Night At The Odeon* matches the archival 2014 release *Live At The Rainbow '74* for raw rock intensity and charismatic stage derring-do from both May and Mercury. The concert has an epic flow and works as a thumbnail sketch of the band from its inception onward. This is classic '70s Queen, four slim longhaired gents in white pearlized satin bell-bottomed jumpsuits, performing with brute energy and swanlike grace; a band in complete control of its sound, able to bend any song or audience to its will."

Classic Rock Revisited's Jeb Wright wrote: "In this show Mr. Mercury shines. He thrived on the big stage and he belonged in this type of original band. The only time one can take his or her eyes off of Freddie is when the lanky Brian May goes forth to do things on his guitar that were cutting edge in 1975. May unleashes his skills and unique guitar tone in front of the audience on 'Now I'm Here', 'Liar' and 'The March Of The Black Queen'.' Together, the band knocks out the classic 'Killer Queen' and proceed to destroy 'Keep Yourself Alive'. At the end of the day, this was a concert that is so good it will find its way back into your living room time after time after time. This was the real Queen, scratching and clawing their way to the top in an uncompromising and triumphant manner."

2016 saw Queen + Adam Lambert embarking on a tour of Europe, Asian called the Queen + Adam Lambert 2016 Summer Festival Tour. They headlined the Isle Of Wight Festival in the UK on June 12.

In a press statement May said: "I think Queen at the Isle of Wight festival is a date that was long overdue. How incredible to take on this challenge at this point in our lives. With an injection of new blood in the shape of the incredible Adam Lambert, Queen will be ready to tear it up on this legendary stage in 2016. Freddie would have loved it. Can't wait."

Taylor continued: "When I think of the Isle of Wight festival, I think of Hendrix, Dylan and the Who. What immortal company to be in. Queen are thrilled to be there and can promise a special night."

And Lambert added: "I'm so excited to be a part of the Isle of Wight Festival and share the stage once again with the Queen family. I adore making music with Roger and Brian, and am thrilled to help continue their legacy into 2016. It is true I have large shoes to fill, so I'm urgently planning on searching for a new pair of boots – or five – to wear for the set."

They performed 'Who Wants To Live Forever; which was dedicated to the victims of the mass shooting at a gay club in Orlando that same day.

The Daily Telegraph's James Hall wrote: "The sheer quality and enduring appeal of the songs trounced all cynicism. And in Lambert they have a charismatic and unique frontman who, to his credit, acknowledged early on that there is only one Freddie Mercury ('You're all thinking it,' he said)."

Ewan Palmer of the *International Business Times* enthused: "From opener 'One Vision' to 'Somebody to Love' and 'I Want To Break Free', each song was widely appreciated by the crowd and at one point I had to begrudgingly admit maybe Queen and Lambert have put on the greatest show of the entire weekend."

They performed in Tel-Aviv in Israel for the first time in front of 58,000 fans.

Further concert material was issued with the release of *On Air*; BBC radio sessions and radio recordings.

AllMusic's Stephen Thomas Erlewine wrote: "Queen can still wander into amorphous territory – 'It's Late' descends into echoing mush - but their muscle seems defined, as does their camp: by ending the set with 'My Melancholy Blues', there's no question that Queen is arch, delivering each of their tunes with a wink. Such revelations are interesting, but the relatively limpness of *Queen On Air* does mean it's an archival release designed only for fans."

Kevin Wierzbicki of *Anti-music* wrote: "One of the real

treats of this 2-CD collection is a version of 'We Will Rock You' that most fans probably have never heard; a fast and punchy punk rock-tinged rocker that sounds nothing like the rhythmically-thumping original. As with everything here, the cut was recorded for BBC Radio in 1973-75 and is otherwise unreleased... The late Queen lead singer Freddie Mercury shouts 'Alright!' at the conclusion of the previously-mentioned 'fast' version of 'We Will Rock You'; fans taking home any version of *Queen On Air: The Complete BBC Radio Sessions* will likely be doing some joyful shouting too."

Singing with KISS and Queen on *Idol* proved that he has the chops to sing rock music, so much so that he fronted Queen in 2012 and then on a major tour of the world in 2014 and 2015 onwards, which pretty much made him a household name the world over. It certainly broadened his appeal in the UK. Critics and fans raved about his performances.

Queen fans were initially dubious, though, about the band hiring a talent show runner-up to front their beloved Queen especially as the collaboration Queen and former Free and Bad Company singer Paul Rodgers didn't go down so well. It has to be said, Queen are not the only major rock band to hire tribute singers or talent show winners and the like; Judas Priest and Journey are just two examples. But Queen have picked the right man for the job this time around. Having seem them live I can attest to that. He's no Freddie Mercury, but he is not meant to be. Neither are they a tribute band. I was blown away by the band's performance and Lambert's showmanship at the Manchester date in the UK in January 2015. He has the voice, the image and the theatrics to perform Queen songs with aplomb. My only criticism is that he is not a seasoned enough performer to have authority over such large audiences, but of course that will come in time. Hopefully there will be more Q+AL tours; and even an album at some point.

In February 2017 the band appeared on *The Late Late Show With James Corden*. Corden and Lambert had an amusing "sing off" to see who would be the better Queen frontman. A North American tour was announced for the summer of '17.

Queen + Adam Lambert 2017 North American Tour:

6/23 — Phoenix, AZ — Gila River Arena

6/24 — Las Vegas, NV — T-Mobile Arena

6/26 — Los Angeles, CA — Hollywood Bowl

6/29 — San Jose, CA — SAP Center

7/01 — Seattle, WA — Key Arena

7/02 — Vancouver, BC — Pepsi Live at Rogers Arena

7/04 — Edmonton, AB — Rogers Place

7/06 — Denver, CO — Pepsi Center Arena

7/08 — Omaha, NE — CenturyLink Center

7/09 — Kansas City, MO — Sprint Center

7/13 — Chicago, IL — United Center

7/14 — St. Paul, MN — Xcel Energy Center

7/17 — Montreal, QC — Bell Centre

7/18 — Toronto, ON — Air Canada Centre

7/20 — Detroit, MI — The Palace of Auburn Hills

7/21 — Cleveland, OH — Quicken Loans Arena

7/23 — Uncasville, CT — Mohegan Sun Arena

7/25 — Boston, MA — TD Garden

7/26 — Newark, NJ — Prudential Center

7/28 — New York, NY — Barclays Center

7/30 — Philadelphia, PA — Wells Fargo Center

7/31 — Washington D.C. — Verizon Center

8/02 — Nashville, TN — Bridgestone Arena

8/04 — Dallas, TX — American Airlines Center

8/05 — Houston, TX — Toyota Center

Queen + Adam Lambert Rocks.

PHOTOS BY CHRIS MEE

PHOTO BY CHRIS MEE

PHOTOS BY CHRIS MEE

PHOTOS BY CHRIS MEE

PHOTOS BY CHRIS MEE

PHOTOS BY CHRIS MEE

PHOTO BY CHRIS MEE

NEIL DANIELS

PHOTOS BY CHRIS MEE

APPENDICES

BRIAN MAY IN HIS OWN WORDS

Intelligent, opinionated yet softly spoken, Brian May usually has something worthwhile to say. Here are some quotes from the press.

"I suppose we were quite an intellectual group, so we would always have lots of discussions about things that weren't music. The music itself is very challenging, so I've never really felt the lack of stimulation."

- **Brian May talking to Ben Mitchell, *Guitar World*, 2013**

"I like the sounds used by The Prodigy, but the truth is I don't like a lot of it. To me it's machines and it's so repetitive that my brain turns off. As for rap, I like a small percentage. I hate the sexist and racist stuff, I find it obnoxious and I don't want any part of it. I get tapes in the post of people who want to make rap songs out of 'We Will Rock You', and they have the most objectionable words in them. We get a number of requests every week and we give permission if we like them – which is almost always."

- **Brian May talking to May Flowers,** *Sydney Morning Herald,* **1998**

"There's a fine line between being very commercial and without any depth on one side, and being totally academic and not relating to people on the other. I have a great interest in operating in this area which is almost art for art's sake, but you are speaking to people and you care whether they buy it or not. I want them to feel something. I want it to do something for them, which, thank God, it normally seems to."

- **Brian May talking to Maura Sutton,** *Classic Rock,* **1998**

"I don't really think about Queen when I get up in the morning these days. It's been a long time and I'm very happy to be away from it. I gave it my all when it was there you know, and it was my life, you know – very proud of what we did – but these days my heads in a another place and I don't really think about um, does this fit in with Queen because it's not my life any more. I just get up and I think, 'Is this any good, does it mean something, and will able to enjoy taking this out on the road?'

That's, that's basically what, what goes through my head, I think. So the same, I have the same commitment to quality as I had with, with Queen, and I wouldn't let anything go out unless I thought it was absolutely there. Which is probably why it takes me so damn long to make things. (laughs) But I'm not gauging it by, you know, does this fit in with Queen fans, 'cos Queen fans are very understanding I find on the whole."

- **Brian May talking to Richard Allinson, *BBC Radio 2*, 1998**

"My concept of a live event is the possibility that can happen everything, without notice. From this point arrive all excitation and energies of the case. You can make mistakes, you can stop in the middle of a song, begin again, improvise. Make your own sound much modern isn't a crime, the important thing is keeping your own style. I'm not a living museum, I like to keep a contact with the things that happen outside my musical vision, without having any fears if my record doesn't look trendy. I can understand what teenagers find interesting in Prodigy, I can understand why my daughter likes Backstreet Boys, without having the same sound."

- **Brian May talking to Tiziano Toniutti,** *Musica Magazine,* **1998**

"There were no limits. Our heroes were The Beatles and Jimi Hendrix, things like *The White Album* were religious texts for us, in terms of how free and creative you can be. And we had better toys than The Beatles had. The studio had developed: we were like artists let loose with loads of lovely paint pots. It's hard to put a name to it. It's just four guys making the music of their passion."

- **Brian May talking to Neil McCormick,** *The Telegraph,* **2011**

"I'm funding a project that's going to increase the amount of surveillance we do on dark objects that might be heading towards us. A few months ago, we were all looking at this object that came between us and the moon, and while we were all watching that, something hit Russia, which was completely unseen and unexpected. It ought to be a wake-up call. That was a pretty big object."

- **Brian May talking to David Browne,** *Rolling Stone,*

2013

"I was an only child. I've always been looking for that thing that can get rid of the loneliness. That's a big part of it. You play to thousands of people, and there's a fantastic energy, you feel good – but then you go home to your hotel room, and you've got yourself to deal with again, and there is a great loneliness."

- **Brian May talking to Rachel Cooke, *The Guardian*, 2010**

"I haven't found it that easy to accustom myself to the new stuff. A lot of the music which Freddie and John want to do is more R&B oriented, and it's hard for me to do that because my playing is a reaction to that style, in a sense. I used to listen to people plucking away on Motown records, and I really didn't like it. I always thought to myself, 'That's the kind of thing I don't want to play. I want the guitar to be up there speaking'. So in a way the return to that was difficult to me. It was a discipline which I gradually worked into, but I find myself wanting to burst out of it all the time and make a lot of noise."

- **Brian May talking to Jas Obrecht, *Guitar Player*, 1983**

"We've all been hauled through the tabloids now. It's very strange that we've been moderately famous for some time, but not tabloid fodder until the last three years. It's not been pleasant. Some papers want a certain kind of news, and it can wreck people's lives. I don't those papers have any sense of responsibility about it."

- **Brian May talking to Paul Elliott, *Sounds*, 1989**

"I wanted to make this record on my own, with nobody else to argue with, just to see what happened. My major driving force really is to do something worthwhile, so that when I do die I can say I'm proud of that. The worst thing you can do is stick out more wallpaper for the world. I would hate to put anything out that I thought was just repetition or superfluous or whatever. The only reason I've put this [*Back To The Light*] out is because I think I actually do have something to say, and it's worth saying. That's why it's taken five years, I suppose, I could have chucked out all sorts of stuff. I'm quite good at being a craftsman, I can make pop songs to a certain extent, I know I can. But I wanted this album to be... to be special to some people."

- **Brian May talking to Kirk Blows, *RCD Magazine*, 1992**

"The reason I wrote 'We Will Rock You' and Freddie [Mercury] wrote 'We Are The Champions' is we enjoyed having that two-way interaction with an audience and that was quite new in those days. These days it's the norm for people to do that and involve the crowd. But back in the '70s, if you look at the context, most rock groups would go out and play really loud to an audience who would listen but not really react that much. They wouldn't really give back that much."

- Brian May talking to Ken Sharp, *Rock Cellar*, 2014

"We went to see The Who one night, and the support act was Jimi Hendrix. It was really an unbelievable experience. The support group situation never changes. Jimi didn't have a sound check, his gear wasn't working properly and his amp kept cutting out. He was getting really embarrassed, but amidst all that he was unbelievable. It was beyond anything I could imagine. I had to revise everything I felt about guitar. I just couldn't believe how good he was. I became a disciple in the course of a few minutes. Then The Who came on – our heroes – and they had a terrible time. They just looked so – I don't even like to say it. You hurt for them because it was impossible to follow Jimi. I still have this great regard for Townshend, but I think he would say the same. There was no one on earth who could follow Hendrix. I think that was one of the things that galvanized me: Hendrix made me think, 'I've got to start being adventurous. I haven't been looking far enough into the future. I've got to start seeing what I can really do.' It made me want to be a professional instead of an amateur."

- **Brian May talking to Nuno Benttencourt, *Guitar World*, 1991**

"Yeah, yeah, yeah. Rock stars shouldn't have anything to say about farming. Well, sorry, it's time to wake up. Farming, like every other industry, including mine, has to be open to change or it dies. ... [And] if the price of my glass of milk on the table, or my cheese is the death of possibly hundreds of thousands of badgers, I don't want it. I like me milk, I like me cheese, but the day the first shot is fired by the government against the badgers, I will never drink another drop of milk unless I know it's come from a humane farm."

- **Brian May talking to Aida Edemariam, *The Guardian*, 2012**

"When Freddie died, it was like losing a family member, and we all handled it in different ways. For a time, I really wanted to escape from Queen; I didn't want to know about it. I think that was my grieving process. But I'm very proud of what we did together. My God, we really did go on some interesting excursions! Mostly, it makes me feel good."

-   **Brian May talking to Neil McCormick, *The Telegraph*, 2011**

"I've always been too much of a nice guy, I'm such a pleaser (emphatically). Freddie was never like that. A kid could be waiting outside for five hours, and Freddie would be like, Oh, fuck off, darling, I need my rest. I'm the nice guy who sits there signing everything that's put in front of me. There were a couple of times on my last tour, when I got the flu and I just had to go home otherwise I would have died, but there's always someone who wants just one more picture. I do try my best but there are times when you have to say, Enough."

-   **Brian May talking to Mark Blake, *Q Magazine*, 1998**

"You spend a lot of time as a songwriter – if I dare call myself a songwriter – living with a song. During that living period where it's growing, it changes and you're aware that, if you pin it down too much, you're destroying it."

- **Brian May talking to Simon Bradley, *Guitarist*, 1998**

"Heavy metal is a strange thing. There's a lot of bravado to heavy metal. I think we're all kind of afraid of women to a certain extent. Even the most heterosexual of us. And heavy metal tends to be a kind of safe place where you can make bold statements about 'what you did with your chick last night.' It's a nice, simple world. It's full of loud stuff and heavy things and strong statements. That's why it's such a great release for chaps, isn't it? I love it. AC/DC is complete therapy. You go to the show and you're deaf for a week. It's wonderful. I'm desperately sad that I had to miss a Black Sabbath reunion show recently. It was Black Sabbath and the Foo Fighters, who I love. And Pantera, who I also love. Unfortunately, I had to be someplace else."

- **Brian May talking to LouAnn Lucero, *Guitar World*, 1998**

NEIL DANIELS

ROCK SCRIBES ON QUEEN

Though Queen were not darlings of the critics during their reign as rock champions, they are far more critically well-received these days. Here are the opinions on Queen from fellow rock writers.

ANDY BRAILSFORD (*FIREWORKS*): "Over the past few years, my partner and I have had a few chuckles at Brian May's expense because, no matter what the event is, be it a tribute concert, a night of 100 Fensons, the Queen's Buckingham Palace gutters being blocked, or the opening of the new local recycling centre; anywhere in fact that there will be free sandwiches, Tizer and pork scratchings, Brian will be there. The thing is, assuming he doesn't just turn up of his own accord and gatecrash, all of the organisers of these events must have invited him. And why is that? Simple. The guy has been in the music business for 46 years now, over which time it is estimated he has sales of over 300 million with his name on. Not bad from somebody who did that playing a self-made guitar, built from an old fireplace, whose sound is instantly recognisable when you hear it. Have a look on the Internet, and you will find plaudits and recognition from all the top guitarists out there, most of them lining up to work with him, if they haven't already.

Brian is also very down to earth, (even though he is a qualified astrophysicist), something I learned when I first met him after a show on *The Works* tour in September 1984. He was more than happy to stand and chat, and share a few secrets only known to him. The same applied to all the subsequent meetings, and other people who have met him will know what I mean when I say, he doesn't seem to change. He is just Brian, which is demonstrated by the fact that he doesn't dye his hair to look younger. (Good lad)! In fact, I have just seen an advertising brochure for a local venue that will be staging Monty Python's *Spamalot*, in which you can choose one from six people to appear as God, on screen during the show, and Brian is one of them. How highly can you be regarded? And he is the only one that doesn't need a wig!!

As far as Queen goes, Brian is very much like Freddie Mercury, in the fact that you could not take him away from the mix and not know he had gone, both from a technical and tonal perspective. He has done a few things over the last few years, but nothing sustained, having only done, (as far as I know), two solo tours since the demise of Queen with Freddie, which is a shame, and a tour last year with Kerry Ellis.

Of course, there are the Queen tours with guest vocalists, and people do say that it is not really Queen without Freddie, or John Deacon who has retired from the music business, and they may be right. But at least it gives us the chance to hear Brian play the songs that established him as one of the world's best guitarists, with the sound he used to do it. Long live Brian."

BAILEY BROTHERS (*ROCK UNITED*): "Anyone who has ever met Brian May will tell you what a nice gentle guy he is. I remember when we all did a tribute concert for Cozy Powell (Buxton, May 1 1999 'A Night To Remember') Brian came over before the show for a chat. He seemed very emotional. It was weird looking at Cozy Powell's kit lit up on stage knowing we are never gonna see him play it ever again. You only have to look at the dignified way Queen handled the illness and eventual death of Freddie Mercury to know these guys have respect for their friends and band mates. Mercury was a total one off, a formidable frontman with an amazing voice but take nothing away from the rest of the band whose vocal harmonies, musicianship and songwriting was a huge part of the Queen sound. To go solo and front your own band is always a daunting task but it can also give you the freedom to create your own music and style. Brian has a high vocal range that can sound a little thin at times but he still knows how to pen a cool rock song; 'Driven By You', I think this is one of the first solo songs the Bailey Brothers remember hearing from Brian taken from the *Back To The Light* album, it was used for a Ford car TV commercial and we kept thinking this is good I wonder who it is because he sounds like Brian May? Then the video came out, it was a great promotional tool and the song was a success. If I had to pick a stand out song from May it would be 'Resurrection' that features Cozy Powell on drums and Neil Murray on bass. This awesome partnership have played in a few bands together including Whitesnake and Black Sabbath, both were very sort-after musicians in the rock world. There's a real energy to this song, it kicks off with a melodic lead guitar intro, it's up tempo and May utilises all his vocal experience gained from being in Queen to add layers of harmonies. The catchy melodic guitar intro is repeated in between verses, there's a cool little moment when you really hear the dynamics from Cozy and an interesting middle 8 section. The only thing that doesn't really fit into the May mould is the second lead guitar solo where he's using a string tapping technique. It's a bit repetitive and not really what you come to expect from Brian, if anything you don't get that signature harmonised guitar sound till the end of the song.

This band did go out on the road supporting Guns N' Roses. I believe, according to Neil, they did have to use female backing singers to assist on those backing vocals but it was a pretty kick ass band. How can you sum up the influence Brian May and Queen have had on the world music scene? Well when your eight year old daughter comes home from school singing all the words to 'Killer Queen', a song penned 32 years before she was born, that shows you how relevant those songs are today. It made the hairs stands out on the back of my neck, and then she's singing 'Bohemian Rhapsody' and 'We Are The Champions' asking me all about the band and searching for their music on her iPod. They had been doing a production of 'We Will Rock You' at her school. Freddie Mercury would have been proud to know that new fans were finding Queen music and that they are still influences young kids and budding musicians to this day.

Brian May took a bit of a risk (and a bit of flack) working with former N-Dubz rapper Dappy on the song 'Rockstar' but personally I don't feel any artist should be shackled by the chains of genre. It was the second single from Dappy's debut album *Bad Intentions*. Brian unleashes a really cool guitar solo at the end of the song. Did the song need it? Not really; it works as a commercial offering but May's melodic ear once again found the icing on the cake. Artists should have the freedom to express themselves with whoever they want to collaborate with and May always comes across truly professional. Many fans sometimes question why artistes in successful bands bother doing solo albums? Well, in a band your input may be limited, you can be restricted creatively and sometimes you just need to show another side to your song writing.

Any guitar player will tell you it's hard to sound original but with a guitar he built and customised himself, you instantly know it's Brian May playing. He keeps it pretty simple and he's not trying to re-invent the wheel but he and drummer Roger Taylor keep the Queen rock 'n' roll wheels turning which is great for the fans. They start 2015 with another massive tour as Queen with Adam Lambert who was a runner up in the eight series of *American Idol*. The Queen machine is over 40 years old but still is as reliable as ever. Brian May is a top bloke and a true professional."

KIRK BLOWS (*AUTHOR*): "'I'm not normal,' confided Brian May candidly, flicking through the pages of a book depicting Queen's illustrious career in the presence of this writer. 'All this has definitely had an effect on me.'

In musical terms, at least, rock fans should be eternally grateful that May is anything but 'normal'. His distinctive, trademark guitar sound is as instantly recognisable as those famous curly locks that caress the sides of his face. But while it has influenced many – his string 'n' sixpence sonics, not his hair – it can never be accurately replicated. That's because May plays and writes with a sincerity and integrity that makes everything he creates uniquely his own. His work has sophistication, substance and, above all, *style*. The proof that he is not prepared to stick out simple 'wallpaper' is reflected in the fact he has produced just two studio albums and one soundtrack under his own name in more than 20 years. His solo output will always exist in the giant shadow of Queen, partly because of the number of band-related projects he's been involved with since their original demise. May is rightly proud of his royal legacy and is reluctant to say goodbye to the past, despite many being tempted to put their feet up. But that's what some 'normal' people would probably do."

NIKK GUNNS (*GET READY TO ROCK*): "A regular in 'Best Guitarist' polls, Brian May will be forever known as the curly haired guitar player in one of the world's best loved rock bands. Outside of Queen, for whom he still keeps the flames burning, he is much more than that.

Campaigner of animal rights, recognised astrophysicist and often overlooked solo artist. However, when I think of Brian May the first thing that comes to mind is the appearance on the roof of Buckingham Palace during the Queen's (that's Elizabeth the II and not the band!!) Golden Jubilee concert in 2002. The second is clogs – I personally have never seen it but have heard that these are his chosen model of footwear, deep down I hope it's not just a myth.

May's solo output is surprisingly just two solo albums, 1992's *Back To The Light* and 1998's *Another World*, plus the soundtrack album *Furia* released in 2000. However, these stand tall amongst some of his best work with Queen. However, his live work as a solo artist dates back to 1982 and since 1998 this seems to have been overtaken by collaborations with other artists – the most successful being with singer Kerry Ellis."

ANDREW HAWNT (*POWERPLAY*): "The defining Brian May moment for me wasn't a Queen moment, oddly. I have vivid memories (and the original TV broadcast on a VHS tape somewhere) of the rock guitar event at the 1992 Sevilla expo (which actually took place in October 1991). Brian May was performing that night with an amazing backing band which featured drum god Cozy Powell, but he also presented the event and acted as an MC, introducing artists and jamming on their tunes.

Other people on stage that night were Joe Satriani, Steve Vai, Joe Walsh and both Gary Cherone and Nuno

Bettencourt from Extreme, and the show was a literal extravaganza of gorgeous guitar work. Vai did his thing, Satriani did it too, Extreme did 'More Than Words', Joe Walsh did 'Rocky Mountain Way' and holding it all together was Brian.

The broadcast showcased two tracks where he took centre stage, namely Queen's 'Now I'm Here' and his big solo hit at the time, 'Driven By You', otherwise known as 'that song from that advert'. While he was massively outgunned in a technical sense by pretty much everyone else playing that night, Brian commanded attention for the simple fact that his playing is so very, very unique.

Nobody sounds like Brian May but Brian May. Aside from the trademark tone and the home made guitar, there's a quality to the phrasing he uses, the structure of the lead parts and the deceptive simplicity of his rhythm playing. On a stage full of guitar legends busily being legendary, Brian was still audible and instantly recognisable.

That's one of his greatest gifts, aside from the big hair and scrawny frame, it's his sound which has always set him apart from the crowd. In a genre of music which can be at times rather interchangeable, Brian May is Brian May and sounds like

Brian May."

GREG PRATO (*ROLLING STONE*): "I've never kept it a secret that Queen is my all-time favourite rock 'n' roll band. And the reason is simple – it's downright extraordinary how many classic tunes the band has offered up through the years (and there are plenty of lesser-known tunes that I feel are on par with the 'We Are The Champions' of their catalog). But even more impressive is the fact that each member is responsible for penning at least one tune that is automatically recognizable by the average bloke on the street. Case in point, 'Bohemian Rhapsody' by Mr. Mercury, 'We Will Rock You' by Mr. May, 'Another One Bites The Dust' by Mr. Deacon, and 'Radio Ga Ga' by Mr. Taylor. As far as its member's solo output goes, I feel the same way as I do about the solo material by many other notable rock acts (Rolling Stones, Led Zeppelin, KISS, etc.) – it is not nearly as strong as a full-on band track, which is a tribute to how special the chemistry of getting all four Queen members together in a room, and having them work on and improve each other's ideas. I have – for the most part – listened regularly to Queen since 1980, and I can honestly say that their music sounds as great today as it did way back yonder. And that, dear friends, is why the original Queen line-up gets my vote for the greatest rock band of all time."

JASON RITCHIE (*GET READY TO ROCK*): "Brian May's two solo albums from the 1990s, *Back To The Light* and *Another World*, are a 'must have' in any Queen fans collection as they show his more rockier side, although there are a couple of ballads that he does so well. His band at the time included top draw musicians like Neil Murray and the late, great Cozy Powell who really gets to show his drumming skills on the excellent 'Resurrection'. His live album recorded at the Brixton Academy back in 1994 is one of the few live albums I really enjoy listening to.

The good thing about Brian May is that he isn't afraid to work with any musician or outside the musical sphere and does not worry about what fans may think! He's had a number one with comedians Hale & Pace, been involved in the excellent but sadly often forgotten about *Starfleet* album and recently with the legendary Tangerine Dream and rapper Dappy. You get to hear a whole host of different musical styles and of course you would not be expected to enjoy them all, however each one features that distinctive guitar sound of Brian May.

He comes across as quiet and thoughtful interviews, however you can see his passion come through in the music he creates and plays, and along with Roger Taylor has kept the name of Queen alive since the passing of Freddie Mercury. Cynics may say they sometimes exploit the Queen name, however they always put on a show and the music of Queen is always foremost.

Brian May for me will always be one of the greatest guitarists of all time and he has been often imitated, but never bettered."

STEVE SWIFT (*POWERPLAY*): "'Starfleet, Starfleet..'; Brian May? Solo? And a theme from a *Terrahawks* competitor? Oh yes, it was a shock when his EP came out in 1983 firstly because he'd always been seen as Queen and Queen alone and also because it was so good. But then B May has been more than Queen, he's been a musician on a search for new sounds.

The dark beauty of *A Day At The Races*, the grandiosity of *News Of The World*, the wonderful oddness of *Jazz* and much,

much more, so much comfort and envelope pushing in equal measure.

But if you want experimentation, look no further than that 1982 album, the fan – dividing *Hot Space.* A disco album. It may have been Freddie and Roger pushing for this, but Brian went for it too, his 'Dancer' a funky strut, his 'Put Out The Fire' containing one of the nastiest solos he ever played – check out that screaming high note!

It is tempting to see May as the bubble haired old rocker and some of the re-re-rereleases of old material might endorse that view.

But there is more; always grounded to allow Freddie to do his thing, he nevertheless delivered air guitar flash by the truckload and surprising moments of absolute musicianly exploration. The coin plectrum, the Carved guitar, the plaintive voice (check out ''39'!) that's all documented; what isn't often mentioned are the chances he took.

He is keeper of the Queen flame.

He did do that album with Paul Rodgers.

But this is a sideshow; the main event is his place as a musician, a musician who can't stand still, a musician who needs to play.

How long may he reign?"

ASSORTED REVIEWS

What follows are a few select reviews from various publications the author has written for over the years. They don't necessarily represent his views in 2015. Opinions change, constantly…

CDs

QUEEN – *LIVE AT THE BOWL* (EMI)

Queen's history as a phenomenally successful live band has been well documented but it does come as a surprise to learn that until now they had only released three live albums: 1979's *Live Killers*, *Live At Wembley* which was recorded on the Magic (and what was to be their final) Tour in 1986 as well as the fairly lacklustre *Live Magic* compilation, also taken from the Magic Tour.

Live At The Bowl was recorded at Milton Keynes' Bowl, June 5, 1982 during a tricky spot in Queen's career. It was part of the tour to promote their David Bowie produced album *Hot Space,* which was to be Queen's attempt at electro-pop or a "funk, black category" as Freddie puts it before they burst into 'Staying Power'. It does seem more than a trifle out of place in between more traditional Queen songs like 'Play The Game' and 'Somebody To Love'. Other than the excellent 'Under Pressure' forget duds like 'Back Chat' and 'Action This Day' from *Hot Space* and this is a terrific live album. It has a hard rock, raw edge as demonstrated on the *Live Killers* album but with better sound quality as opposed to the mid-'80s slick, pop-friendly rock of *Live At Wembley*.

Amongst 25 songs both the fast and slow, heavier version of 'We Will Rock You' is present as are live goodies like 'Now I'm Here', 'Tie Your Mother Down' and 'Sheer Heart Attack' which all show Queen's tremendous live ability in full flight. We are also treated to killer versions of 'Fat Bottomed Girls', 'Dragon Attack' and 'Save Me'.

With Freddie's powerful vocal performance, the band's professional delivery and the enthusiastic audience plus the fact that this has never been released before on CD, *Live At The Bowl* will please most fans who still crave live material from the royalty of British rock.

QUEEN & PAUL RODGERS – *THE COSMOS ROCKS* (EMI)

This has to be one of the year's most anticipated rock albums yet there has been surprisingly little hype in the mainstream for such a huge band.

When it was announced in 2004 that Queen and the revered blues singer/rock journey man Paul Rodgers were going to unite for world tour in 2005, well, a lot of people were perplexed. *Hmmm….how is this going to work out?.*

The tour proved to be a big success and the reviews were, for the most part, surprisingly good. I went to the Manchester show and quite enjoyed it although I was a bit disappointed about the set and still think songs like 'I Want To Break Free' just don't work for Rodgers' voice; but a lot of the early seventies stuff like 'Tie Your Mother Down' was brilliantly played. Mid-2006 and Brian May announced plans for a brand new studio album bearing the Queen name and logo; the first Queen album since *Made In Heaven* which came out four years after Freddie Mercury's death in 1991. Again, some fans expressed a nervousness about the prospect of a new Queen album without Freddie Mercury but the key here is that it is

Queen *and* Paul Rodgers. But then it's not really Queen, is it?
It's half of Queen because bassist John Deacon is fully retired.
Projects like this will always cause debate and divide fans but
the point is: here is a new studio album so enjoy the fact that
Brian May and Roger Taylor are working together again.

The big question is: does *The Cosmos Rocks* have the
classic Queen sound? Yes, most of it does. There's plenty of
room for Rodgers to do his thing while Taylor brings in those
wonderful melodic harmonies and backing vocals; and May
brings his trademark riffs and solos into the mix. The production
is vibrant and modern but of course, they were never going to
settle for anything less than top-notch.

Unfortunately at the time of writing I had no sleeve
notes to elaborate on backing musicians and so forth but I can
say that the trio of Rodgers, Taylor and May sounds terrific.

The title-track, which happens to be the opening song,
starts with some production effects before the unmistakable
guitars of Brian May builds up the tempo and the band spring
into action…along with some clapping. 'C-lebrity' is an
interesting song; written by Taylor, it is about the current trend
of people appearing on shows like *Big Brother* and becoming

famous simply for being in front of the camera rather than having any discernible talent. The backing vocals work well and the chorus is memorable but May's solo is a little too short. 'Surf's Up…School's Out' is an odd one; it could easily fit on something like 'Sheer Heart Attack'. This version of 'Say It's Not True' is better then what I've heard before as all three share lead vocals. 'Call Me' is the quirky sing-a-long acoustic ballad that could easily be as popular as something like 'Crazy Little Thing Called Love'. The weakest track may actually be the ballad 'Through The Night'. 'War Boys' is a sturdy rocker and 'Time To Shine' has some interesting arrangements.

It's not as heavy as I would have liked but the classic Queen trademarks are here, spread across the 14 tracks. Overall, if you can get used to a difference in vocals and a mix of two uniquely different artists, each with their own identity ('Voodoo' is more of a Rodgers track,) then you'll really enjoy this album.

The Cosmos Rocks takes some getting used to but it's a grower. It certainly has some strong and consistent material.

Oh, and there are various editions available: I've opted for the CD/DVD version.

Has the wait been worth it? Is it good enough to bear

the Queen name and logo? Yes to both. There's some strong material here. It's a grower.

BOOKS

LAURA JACKSON – *BRIAN MAY: THE DEFINITIVE BIOGRAPHY* (Portrait)

Jackson has written previous books on Brian May and Queen (as well as books on Bon Jovi and a host of celebrities) so she could be classed as an "expert". Brian May is a number of things: a hugely gifted guitarist, an intelligent person with a PhD in Astronomy/Physics and an accomplished songwriter.

Jackson sheds light on his pre-Queen life and the connection between Queen and my hometown St. Helens (Lancashire) during the early years is especially interesting from a personal viewpoint.

During the Queen years, Jackson seems more interested in Freddie Mercury than she does with the main subject but the author does rightly argue that May was the "father figure" in the band which is backed up by Def Leppard's Joe Elliott, a major Queen fan and friend of May's. And since Mercury's death, May has been the one to steer the band toward further success whilst also alienating bassist John Deacon and making a few wrong turns such as the needless release of *Greatest Hits III*.

Jackson is also a little light on the Rodgers/Queen collaboration and the author fails to mention May's brilliant online diary 'Soapbox'. Having said that, the author's passion for May and Queen is clearly enthusiastic and her writing style is clear and concise.

Anything that uses the Queen name sells but like other major bands Queen/May has a hugely obsessive fan base so this book may only appeal to the casual fan.

PHIL SUTCLIFFE – *QUEEN: THE ULTIMATE ILLUSTRATED HISTORY OF THE CROWN KINGS OF ROCK* (Voyageur Press)

Certainly some of the decisions Brian May and Roger Taylor have made since Freddie Mercury's death in 1991 have been dubious to say the least but the short-lived Paul Rodgers collaboration, the *We Will Rock You* musical and the band's appearances on *The X Factor* and *American Idol* have brought a whole new legion of fans to the Queen camp.

Sure, a majority of people will associate Queen with their big stadium rock anthems rather than the majesty of their earlier material so what respected rock scribe Phil Sutcliffe has done is give a handy overview of the band's entire career.

There are no revelations or anything like that; it's merely a history of the band that's well written and informative. I consider myself to be a Queen fan and some of the visual material in this book is absolutely stunning. It's a heavy hardback that weighs a ton and is filled to the brim with great visual treats like ticket stubs, posters and assorted bits of memorabilia. There are tour dates, press articles and album reviews.

The photographs of the band offstage – especially those with Freddie at home or with friends – are revealing and quite touching. Even without listening to the music, the photographs of the band onstage show them as the rock gods they still are. There is a lot of stuff out there on Queen and Sutcliffe's book is definitely one to pick up.

LIVE

QUEEN + PAUL RODGERS

M.E.N. ARENA, MANCHESTER – MAY 4, 2005

They just can't leave it alone, can they? Of course I'm not talking about retired bassist John Deacon but the ever-restless energy of Brian May and Roger Taylor who cannot appear to settle Queen's memory in peace thus allowing it to garner the reverence it deserves. What, with the unnecessary covers duets with Five and Robbie Williams (Arrr! – let's not talk about that) and the dreadful but bafflingly successful *We Will Rock You* musical you'd think they were short of a bob or two. Taylor and May have always loved the live stage and tonight showed they're relishing being back on the road under the Queen name for the first time since 1986.

It was always down to who could replace Freddie Mercury. Simply nobody can so having ex-Free and Bad Company singer Paul Rodgers take over the vocal reigns is certainly a curious choice. How can a man proclaimed 'the world's best white blues singer' tackle Queen's eclectic back catalogue and carry it off without looking naff?

Opening to a recording of Eminem's 'Lose Yourself' was decidedly perplexing yet as soon as May ripped into the raw riff of 'Tie Your Mother Down' they could be forgiven for such an out of place introduction.

With Queen's roots based firmly in '70s glam rock, what could have been a blistering two-hour set was a largely haphazard cut and paste effort. Rodgers handled vintage songs like 'Fat Bottomed Girls' well enough but his take on '80s chart toppers like 'A Kind Of Magic' and 'I Want To Break Free' was almost embarrassing.

When Rodgers disappeared in mid-set for about forty minutes just what was May and Taylor thinking when they decided to sing some of the songs themselves? May is certainly a wizard on the guitar but his vocals talents have a lot to be desired. He doesn't have the strength to cut into the beef of 'I Want It All' and the slow-down-speeded up version of 'Hammer To Fall' was utter nonsense. Taylor was reasonably apt on 'Radio Ga Ga' but it still failed to shine. May's guitar solo was tediously overlong but Taylor's 'I'm In Love With My Car' was appropriately heavy.

It came as no surprise then that the best songs of the night were Free favourites like 'All Right Now' and 'Wishing Well' and Bad Company's 'Can't Get Enough Of Your Love'. It goes to show that you can get May and Taylor to play other people's songs but you can't cant another singer to sing what Freddie could.

'Under Pressure' was a modest effort but it failed inspire. Having video footage of Freddie singing the opening verses of 'Bohemian Rhapsody' before Rodgers sang the heavy 'middle-bit' was a tribute to the great man more than anything else. Rodgers voice occasionally cracked under the strain especially toward the end with 'We Are The Champions' but there was still a particular chemistry between him and the band.

Without Deacon but with a rhythm guitarist, bassist and piano player it blatantly wasn't Queen. But still, if the setlist was fixed in Queen's awesome seventies repertoire, it could have been a killer queen set but sadly tonight was inconsistent.

NEIL DANIELS

SELECTIVE DISCOGRAPHY

This is a casual list of Queen releases…

QUEEN *(SELECTIVE)*

STUDIO

QUEEN *(EMI, 1973)*

QUEEN II *(EMI, 1974)*

SHEER HEART ATTACK *(EMI, 1974)*

A NIGHT AT THE OPERA *(EMI, 1975)*

A DAY AT THE RACES *(EMI, 1976)*

NEWS OF THE WORLD *(EMI, 1977)*

JAZZ *(EMI, 1978)*

THE GAME *(EMI, 1980)*

FLASH GORDON *(EMI, 1980)*

HOT SPACE *(EMI, 1982)*

THE WORKS *(EMI, 1984)*

A KIND OF MAGIC *(EMI, 1986)*

THE MIRACLE *(EMI, 1989)*

INNUENDO *(EMI, 1991)*

MADE IN HEAVEN *(EMI, 1995)*

LIVE

LIVE KILLERS *(EMI, 1979)*

LIVE MAGIC *(EMI, 1986)*

LIVE AT WEMBLEY '86 *(EMI, 1992)*

QUEEN ON FIRE – LIVE AT THE BOWL *(EMI, 2004)*

QUEEN ROCK MONTREAL *(EMI, 2007)*

HUNGARIAN RHAPSODY: QUEEN LIVE IN BUDAPEST *(Universal, 2012)*

QUEEN: LIVE AT THE RAINBOW '74 *(Universal, 2014)*

A NIGHT AT THE ODEON – HAMMERSMITH 1975 *(Universal, 2015)*

ON AIR *(EMI, 2016)*

COMPILATIONS

GREATEST HITS *(EMI, 1981)*

GREATEST HITS II *(EMI, 1991)*

QUEEN ROCKS *(EMI, 1997)*

GREATEST HITS III *(EMI, 1999)*

ABSOLUTE QUEEN *(EMI, 2009)*

DEEP CUTS, VOLUME I *(Universal, 2011)*

DEEP CUTS, VOLUME II *(Universal, 2011)*

DEEP CUTS, VOLUME III *(Universal, 2011)*

QUEEN FOREVER *(Universal, 2014)*

Some of Brian May's notable compositions for Queen include:

'KEEP YOURSELF ALIVE' *(1973)*

'SOME DAY, ONE DAY' *(1974)*

'SHE MAKES ME (STORMTROOPER IN STILETTOES)' *(1974)*

''39' *(1975)*

'GOOD COMPANY' *(1975)*

'LONG AWAY' *(1976)*

'ALL DEAD, ALL DEAD' *(1977)*

'SLEEPING ON THE SIDEWALK' *(1977)*

'FAT BOTTOMED GIRLS' *(1978)*

'LEAVING HOME AIN'T EASY' *(1978)*

'SAIL AWAY SWEET SISTER' *(1980)*

'FLASH' *(1980)*

'PUT OUT THE FIRE' *(1982)*

'LAS PALABRAS DE AMOR' *(1982)*

'I GO CRAZY' *(1984)*

'WHO WANTS TO LIVE FOREVER' *(1986)*

'I WANT IT ALL' *(1989)*

'LOST OPPORTUNITY' *(1991)*

'MOTHER LOVE' *(1995)*

'LET ME LOVE' *(1995)*

'NO-ONE BUT YOU' *(1997)*

QUEEN + PAUL RODGERS

STUDIO

THE COSMOS ROCKS *(EMI, 2008)*

LIVE

RETURN OF THE CHAMPIONS *(EMI, 2005)*

LIVE IN UKRIANE *(EMI, 2009)*

QUEEN & VARIOUS ARTISTS ASSORTED SINGLES

'SOMEBODY TO LOVE' *(live)*

(Queen + George Michael) (1993)

'ANOTHER ONE BITES THE DUST'

(Queen + Wyclef Jean ft. Pras and Free) (1998)

'WE WILL ROCK YOU'

(5ive + Queen) (2000)

'FLASH'

(Queen + Vanguard) (2003)

'REACHING OUT' / 'TIE YOUR MOTHER DOWN'

(Queen + Paul Rodgers) (2005)

'ANOTHER ONE BITES THE DUST'

(Queen vs. The Miami Project) (2006)

'SAY IT'S NOT TRUE'

(Queen + Paul Rodgers) (2007)

'C-LEBRITY'

(Queen + Paul Rodgers) (2008)

'WE BELIEVE'

(Queen + Paul Rodgers) (2008)

'BOHEMIAN RHAPSODY'

(Queen + The Muppets) (2009)

'WE WILL ROCK YOU VON LICHTEN'

(Queen + Von Lichten) (2012)

HEADLINING TOURS

QUEEN + PAUL RODGERS TOUR *(2005–06)*

ROCK THE COSMOS TOUR *(2008)*

QUEEN + ADAM LAMBERT TOUR 2012 *(2012)*

QUEEN + ADAM LAMBERT TOUR 2014–2015 *(2014–15)*

QUEEN + ADAM LAMBERT 2016 SUMMER FESTIVAL
TOUR *(2016)*

QUEEN + ADAM LAMBERT 2017 NORTH AMERICAN
SUMMER TOUR *(2017)*

TOURING MUSICIANS

SPIKE EDNEY *(keyboards / piano / guitar / backing vocals;*

1984–present)

NEIL FAIRCLOUGH *(bass guitar & backing vocals; 2011–present)*

JAMIE MOSES *(rhythm guitar & backing vocals; 1998–2009)*

DANNY MIRANDA *(bass guitar & backing vocals; 2005–2009)*

RUFUS TIGER TAYLOR *(percussion / drums / backing vocals; 2011–present)*

BOOKS BY

NEIL DANIELS

PUBLISHED BY

CREATESPACE

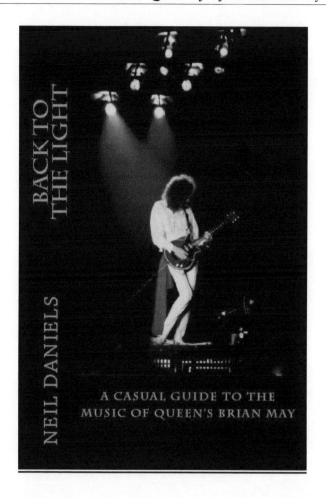

BACK TO THE LIGHT – A CASUAL GUIDE TO THE

MUSIC OF QUEEN'S BRIAN MAY

(CREATESPACE, 2015).

FROM AMERICAN IDOL TO BRITISH ROCK ROYALTY –

THE AMAZING STORY OF ADAM LAMBERT

(CREATESPACE, 2015).

ABOUT THE AUTHOR

NEIL DANIELS has written about rock and metal for a wide range of magazines, fanzines and websites. He has written over a dozen books on such artists as Adam Lambert, Judas Priest, Ace Frehley, Joe Perry, Rob Halford, Bon Jovi, Linkin Park, Journey, Bryan Adams, Neal Schon, Richie Sambora, Brian May, Iron Maiden, You Me At Six, 5 Seconds Of Summer, Metallica, AC/DC, Pantera, UFO, ZZ Top and Robert Plant. He also co-authored *Dawn Of The Metal Gods: My Life In Judas Priest And Heavy Metal* with original Judas Priest singer/co-founder Al Atkins. His third book on Judas Priest is the CD sized *Rock Landmarks – Judas Priest's British Steel*, published by Wymer.

His acclaimed series, *All Pens Blazing – A Rock And Heavy Metal Writer's Handbook Volumes I & II,* collects over a hundred original and exclusive interviews with some of the world's most famous rock and metal scribes.

His second duel collection of rock writings, *Rock 'N' Roll*

Mercenaries – Interviews With Rock Stars Volumes I & II, compiles sixty interviews with many well-known rock stars and scribes. The former collections were republished via Createspace as *Rock 'N' Roll Sinners* while the latter books were republished in an omnibus edition titled, *Hard Rock Rebels – Talking With Rock Stars*.

His Createspace books are *AOR Chronicles*, *Rock & Metal Chronicles, Hard Rock Rebels – Talking With Rock Stars*, *Rock 'N' Roll Sinners – Volumes I, II & III*, *Rock Bites, Love It Loud, Get Your Rock On – Melodic Rock Shots, Bang Your Head – Heavy Metal Shots, In A Dark Room – Exploits Of A Genre Fan* and the fictional rock 'n' roll novel, *It's My Life*.

His books have so far been translated into Brazilian, Bulgarian, Czech, Finnish, French, German, Italian, Japanese, Polish and Swedish with more foreign titles in the works.

His reviews, articles and interviews on rock music and pop culture have been published in *The Guardian, Classic Rock Presents AOR, Classic Rock Presents Let It Rock, Rock Sound*,

Record Collector, *Big Cheese*, *Powerplay*, *Fireworks*,

MediaMagazine, *Rocktopia.co.uk*, *Get Ready To Rock.com*,

Lucemfero.com, *musicOMH.com*, *Ghostcultmag.com*, *Drowned*

In Sound.com, *BBCNewsOnline.co.uk*, *Carling.com*,

Unbarred.co.uk and *Planet Sound* on Channel4's Teletext

service. He has also written several sets of sleeve notes for

Angel Air and BGO Records.

His website is *www.neildanielsbooks.com*

PUBLISHED BOOKS BY NEIL DANIELS

MUSIC BIOGRAPHIES

The Story Of Judas Priest: Defenders Of The Faith

(Omnibus Press, 2007).

Robert Plant: Led Zeppelin, Jimmy Page And The Solo Years

(Independent Music Press, 2008).

Bon Jovi Encyclopaedia

(Chrome Dreams, 2009).

Dawn Of The Metal Gods: My Life In Judas Priest And Heavy Metal **(with Al Atkins)**

(Iron Pages, 2009).

Linkin Park – An Operator's Manual

(Chrome Dreams, 2009).

Don't Stop Believin' – The Untold Story Of Journey

(Omnibus Press, 2011).

Rock Landmarks: Judas Priest's British Steel

(Wymer Publishing, 2011).

Metallica – The Early Years And The Rise Of Metal

(Independent Music Press, 2012).

Iron Maiden – The Ultimate Unauthorised History Of The Beast

(Voyageur Press, 2012).

You Me At Six – Never Hold An Underdog Down

(Independent Music Press, 2012).

AC/DC – The Early Years With Bon Scott

(Independent Music Press, 2013).

Reinventing Metal – The True Story Of Pantera And The Tragically Short Life Of Dimebag Darrell

(Backbeat Books, 2013).

High Stakes & Dangerous Men – The UFO Story

(Soundcheck Books, 2013).

Beer Drinkers & Hell Raisers – A ZZ Top Guide

(Soundcheck Books, 2014).

Killers – The Origins Of Iron Maiden: 1975-1983

(Soundcheck Books, 2014).

Let It Rock – The Making Of Bon Jovi's Slippery When Wet

(Soundcheck Books, 2014).

From American Idol To British Rock Royalty – The Amazing Story Of Adam Lambert

(Createspace, 2015).

Pop Punk From Down Under – The Story Of 5 Seconds Of Summer

(Createspace, 2015).

Big 4 Encyclopedia – A Guide To The Metal Music Of

Metallica, Slayer, Megadeth & Anthrax

(Createspace, 2016).

Judas Priest – A Metal Gods Scrapbook

(Createspace, 2016).

Bon Jovi – A New Jersey Rockers Handbook

(Createspace, 2016).

Judas Priest – A Metal Gods Scrapbook

(Createspace, 2016).

Iron Maiden – Playing With Madness: A Collection Of Writings On The Beast

(Createspace, 2016).

Metallica – A Thrash Metal Salute

(Createspace, 2017).

FILM BIOGRAPHIES

Matthew McConaughey – The Biography

(John Blake, 2014).

The Unexpected Adventures Of Martin Freeman

(John Blake, 2015).

J.J. Abrams – A Study In Genius: The Unofficial Biography

(John Blake, 2015).

CASUAL GUIDES

Electric World – A Casual Guide To The Music Of Journey's Neal Schon

(Createspace, 2014).

Reckless – A Casual Guide To The Music Of Bryan Adams

(Createspace, 2014).

Stranger In This Town – A Casual Guide To The Music Of Bon Jovi's Richie Sambora

(Createspace, 2014).

Made Of Metal – A Casual Guide To The Solo Music Of Judas Priest's Rob Halford

(Createspace, 2014).

Back To The Light – A Casual Guide To The Music Of Queen's Brian May

(Createspace, 2015).

Once A Rocker, Always A Rock – A Casual Guide To The Music Of Aerosmith's Joe Perry

(Createspace, 2015).

Live To Win – A Casual Guide To The Music Of KISS Guitarist Paul Stanley

(Createspace, 2015).

Space Invader – A Casual Guide To The Music Of Original KISS Guitarist Ace Frehley

(Createspace, 2016).

COLLECTED WORKS

All Pens Blazing: A Rock And Heavy Metal Writer's Handbook Volume I

(AuthorsOnline, 2009).

All Pens Blazing: A Rock And Heavy Metal Writer's Handbook Volume II

(AuthorsOnline, 2010).

Rock 'N' Roll Mercenaries – Interviews With Rock Stars Volume I

(AuthorsOnline, 2010).

Rock 'N' Roll Mercenaries – Interviews With Rock Stars Volume II

(AuthorsOnline, 2011).

CREATESPACE

AOR Chronicles – Volume 1

(Createspace, 2013).

Rock & Metal Chronicles – Volume 1

(Createspace, 2013).

Hard Rock Rebels – Talking With Rock Stars

(Createspace, 2013).

Rock 'N' Roll Sinners – Volume I

(Createspace, 2013).

Rock 'N' Roll Sinners – Volume II

(Createspace, 2013).

Rock 'N' Roll Sinners – Volume III

(Createspace, 2013).

Rock Bites

(Createspace, 2013).

Love It Loud

(Createspace, 2013).

Get Your Rock On – Melodic Rock Shots

(Createspace, 2013).

Bang Your Head – Heavy Metal Shots

(Createspace, 2013).

In A Dark Room – Exploits Of A Genre Fan

(Createspace, 2013).

Hard N' Heavy – A Rock Reviews Compilation

(Createspace, 2016).

Heavy Metal Madness – Reviews & Interviews With Metal Bands

(Createspace, 2016).

FICTION

It's My Life – A (Fictional) Rock 'N' Roll Memoir

(Createspace, 2013).

PRAISE FOR THE AUTHOR'S PREVIOUS WORKS

"Neil Daniels is great on the early years of Brummie metal legends Judas Priest..."

- *Classic Rock* on **The Story Of Judas Priest: Defenders Of The Faith**

"'I've never reached the top...but I gave it a bloody good go!' says original Judas Priest singer Al Atkins in the introduction to his autobiography. With a foreword by Judas Priest bassist Ian Hill ... Metal Gods *covers the pre-fame years of the second-ever metal band in entertaining detail".*

- *Metal Hammer* on **Dawn Of The Metal Gods: My Life In Judas Priest And Heavy Metal**

"The book also has a curious appendices exploring – among other things – Percy's interest in folklore and mythology".

- *Mojo* on **Robert Plant: Led Zeppelin, Jimmy Page And The Solo Years**

"Prolific rock and metal author Neil Daniels does a very good

job in detailing a veritable smorgasbord of the events, places, people, release and merchandises of the band, the writer displaying his customary attention to detail and enthusiasm for accuracy".

- *Record Collector* on **Bon Jovi Encyclopaedia**

"...in terms of writing, content and presentation I think it's probably his best... Linkin Park - An Operator's Manual *is an attractive book with black and white photos on every page".*

- *Fireworks* on **Linkin Park – An Operator's Manual**

"... the aggregate of this book is an at minimum interesting and at max fascinating read for any rock fan, 'cos you get the whole deal, the history of Sounds, Kerrang!, Metal Hammer, BW&BK, *all the mags, plus the mechanics of book writing, and more mainstream, who's a good interview and bad plus proof, crazy road stories...friggin' well all of this would be interesting to any rocker. Period".*

- *Bravewords.com* on **All Pens Blazing: A Rock And Heavy Metal Writer's Handbook Volume I**

"But once again, this rollercoaster ride through some of rock's back pages will bring a glow to the cheek, and perhaps even moistness to the mouth, of any self-respecting rock fan who has ever bought a music paper or mag since the 1970s".

- *Get Ready To Rock.com* on **All Pens Blazing: A Rock And Heavy Metal Writer's Handbook Volume II**

"These two volumes of interviews celebrate the art of rock journalism".

- *Classic Rock* on **All Pens Blazing: A Rock And Heavy Metal Writer's Handbook Volumes 1 & 11**

"As a lone-time yet casual fan of the band, I found the band's story very interesting and quite surprising... I received the book on Thursday, used every possible opportunity to read it and finished it on Sunday. That's a recommendation if any".

- *Rock United.com* on **Don't Stop Believin' – The Untold Story Of Journey**

"With a track by track analysis, tour dates and photos from the

period this is everything you needed to know about what is arguably Priest's finest thirty-odd minutes wrapped up into in one handy bite sized paperback at a budget price".

- *Sea Of Tranquility.org* on **Rock Landmarks – Judas Priest's British Steel**

"It's an insightful look at one of metal's most important bands, and though there have been many books written about them, Metallica have never seemed as easy to understand as after reading this".

- *Curled Up.com* on **Metallica – The Early Years And The Rise Of Metal**

"In all, Daniels has crafted a very high-level and easy read with Iron Maiden – The Ultimate Unauthorized History Of The Beast, *and top it all off, it's packaged expertly, prime for your coffee table, where Eddie's piercing eyes await".*

- *Blistering.com* on **Iron Maiden – The Ultimate Unauthorised History Of The Beast**

"This book was a great read. 154 pages crammed with the

wonderfully written story of You Me At Six... With some lovely photos and a very handy discography at the back, You Me At Six – Never Hold An Underdog Down *is a must have for any YMAS fan".*

- *Get Ready To Rock.com* on **You Me At Six – Never Hold An Underdog Down**

"Daniels style is engaging and covers in excellent detail the first six years of the band...Each chapter covers a year and Daniels provides great detail on the various Australian vs. International pressings of the first few albums. It's very detailed and well researched".

- *Metal-Rules.com* on **AC/DC – The Early Years With Bon Scott**

"The tours, the music, the fun, the life, and the death, of one of the best metal acts of the '90s...it's all here. Nice job once again by Mr. Daniels".

- *Sea Of Tranquility.org* on **Reinventing Metal – The True Story Of Pantera And The Tragically Short Life Of Dimebag Darrell**

"Overall, I wouldn't hesitate to recommend this book to not only the diehards (who will snap it up anyway), but also those who want to delve just a little further than Michael Schenker, Phil Mogg (who emerges as quite the dictatorial figure in places), and the band's often horrendous choice of stage outfits!"

- *Classic Rock Society* on **High Stakes & Dangerous Men – The UFO Story**

"The book is an insight into the group's rise to fame, the funny times and their rise to become iconic bearded rocking heroes. I really enjoyed the section on ZZ Top trivia, there's funny and intriguing examples to make you smile and laugh out loud".

- *The Mayfair Mall Zine.com* on **Beer Drinkers & Hell Raisers – A ZZ Top Guide**

"This is a book for the superfan, to be honest. But for the superfan, it is a fantastic volume collecting a ton of information on a great player that you wouldn't be able to find in one place otherwise".

- *Music Tomes.com* on **Electric World – A Casual Guide To The Music Of Journey's Neal Schon**

"...if you thought you knew everything there was to know about Iron Maiden, then think again, as Daniels manages to turn up nugget after nugget of trivia and fact. This is a very rewarding read and I would wholeheartedly recommend this to any rock music fan, in fact buy it now and pack it away in your suitcase for your summer holiday read".

- *Planet Mosh.com* on **Killers – The Origins Of Iron Maiden: 1975-1983**

"Told in straightforward language and amazingly concise as for the time span it covers, Let It Rock: The Making Of Bon Jovi's Slippery When Wet *is a fine, solid work".*

- *Hardrock Heaven* on **Let It Rock – The Making Of Bon Jovi's Slippery When Wet**

"...Mr Daniels has applied his knack of bringing you right into the subject here and Bryan Adams fans will love Reckless - A Casual Guide To The Music Of Bryan Adams*".*

- *Get Ready To Rock* on **Reckless – A Casual Guide To The Music Of Bryan Adams**

"Made Of Metal *is a excellent guide to the long, sometimes magnificent, sometimes frustrating, sometimes downright horrible solo career of the Metal God"*.

- *Metal-Rules* on **Made Of Metal – A Casual Guide To The Solo Music Of Judas Priest's Rob Halford**

VISIT

WWW.NEILDANIELSBOOKS.COM

FOR MORE INFORMATION

NEIL DANIELS

NEIL DANIELS BOOKS

AUTHOR / CRITIC / MUSIC JOURNALIST / WRITER

QUALITY BOOKS ON ROCK & METAL MUSIC AND POP CULTURE

For details on **Neil Daniels Books** visit:

www.neildanielsbooks.com

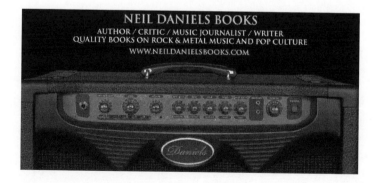

Printed in Great
Britain
by Amazon